T0305951

"The movement for better public engagement with science often focuses on the natural sciences. Macknight and Medvecky have brought together authors who push us to the harder problem: public engagement with SOCIAL sciences. Knowing about economics is probably more fundamental to being an informed and engaged citizen than knowing about physics or biology. This important book opens new opportunities for research and practice in how publics engage with economics."

Bruce Lewenstein, *Professor of Science Communication,*
Departments of Communication and of Science & Technology
Studies, Cornell University

"The stakes are high when it comes to the public discussion of economics. The subject is technical – close to a science – which means setting out an economic decision in a simple and clear way can be hard. But unlike the sciences, economics is hard-wired into policy decisions that affect all of us, every day. *Making Economics Public* shows the huge risks that result – from poorly understood policies to outright dishonesty – and what we must do about it. Each author contributes to establishing the central problem: while we constantly chew over the economy – markets, prices, unemployment – in public debate, discussion of the underlying economics that drive these outcomes is scant. *Making Economics Public* is a bold step towards rectifying this problem, packed with examples of how and why public discourse can be so thin, shallow and opaque, and what can be done about it. The book should be a mandatory read for policy economists and will be an enlightening read for anyone seeking a better understanding of the forces shaping our lives."

Richard Davies, *Professor of the Public Understanding of*
Economics, University of Bristol

MAKING ECONOMICS PUBLIC

Economics – macro, micro and mysterious – is integral to everyday life. But despite its importance for personal and collective decision making, it is a discipline often viewed as technical, arcane and inaccessible and thus overlooked in public discourse. This book is a call to arms to bring the discipline of economics more into the public domain. It calls on economists to think about how to make their knowledge of the economics public. And it calls on those who specialise in communicating expert knowledge to help us learn to communicate about economics. The book brings together scholars and practitioners working at the early stages of an emerging field: the public communication of, and public engagement with, economics. Through a series of short essays from academics and practitioners, the book has two key goals: first and foremost, it will make a case for why we need to make economics public and for the importance of having a clear vision of what it means to make economics public. Secondly, it suggests some ways that this can be done featuring contributions from practitioners, including economists, who are engaging audiences in newspapers, museums and beyond. This book is essential reading for those in economics with an interest in making economics public and those already in the many fields dedicated to communicating expert knowledge in public spaces who have an interest in where economics can fit.

Vicki Macknight works in the Centre for Science Communication at the University of Otago. Her work has been published in a range of journals. She is the author of *Imagining Classrooms: Stories of Children, Teaching and Ethnography* (2016).

Fabien Medvecky is a Senior Lecturer in the Department of Science Communication at the University of Otago. Armed with graduate degrees in Philosophy and Economics, he studies the relationship between knowledge and society and how social interactions shape, create and direct what counts as knowledge. Dr Medvecky is especially interested in areas that are challenging and uncomfortable, from ethical and justice issues in communicating information to questions over contentious or controversial science and technologies (gene tech, alternative medicine, etc.). He also has a long-running interest in how economics (the discipline, not the economy) is made public and how that interacts with other forms of knowledge and expertise.

MAKING ECONOMICS PUBLIC

The Hows and Whys of Communicating Markets and Models

Edited by
Vicki Macknight and
Fabien Medvecky

Routledge
Taylor & Francis Group

LONDON AND NEW YORK

Designed cover image: © Getty Images

First published 2023
by Routledge
4 Park Square, Milton Park, Abingdon, Oxon OX14 4RN

and by Routledge
605 Third Avenue, New York, NY 10158

Routledge is an imprint of the Taylor & Francis Group, an informa business

British Library Cataloguing-in-Publication Data
A catalogue record for this book is available from the British Library

ISBN: 978-1-032-25487-6 (hbk)
ISBN: 978-1-032-25485-2 (pbk)
ISBN: 978-1-003-28344-7 (ebk)

DOI: 10.4324/9781003283447

Typeset in Bembo
by codeMantra

CONTENTS

ILLUSTRATIONS

Figures

Table

CONTRIBUTORS

Kevin Albertson is Professor of Economics at Manchester Metropolitan University with a background in statistics and political economics. Kevin's work ranges from business and social forecasting and the evaluation of government policy to the impact of globalised liberal markets on the political economic prospects of the UK; the ways, means and implications of privatisation and marketisation in the public sector; and the development of social, and responsible, innovation. He is currently working in the areas of employment and society in a low-to-zero (economic) growth economy and the well-being aspects of relational – as opposed to transactional – socio-economic interactions. He is the author/co-author of over 40 refereed academic articles and book chapters, and is a co-author/editor of eight books, including the Haynes Guide, *How to Run the Country*.

Pierre Benz is a postdoctoral researcher at the Institute of Political Studies, University of Lausanne, Switzerland. As a member of the Swiss Elite Observatory, he is involved in the comprehensive analysis of biographical and historical data and develops interdisciplinary research strategies on elites and power. With a PhD in social sciences, the core of his research work focuses on the historical sociology of biological and chemical sciences, social inequalities in science, scientific careers and interdisciplinary collaborations in the natural sciences. More recently, he has conducted research on the Swiss power elite through the study of corporate networks, kinship and spatial inequalities. He recently published in *Higher Education*, *Zilsel* and *Social Science Information*.

Christopher L. Colvin is Senior Lecturer in Economics at Queen's University Belfast, where he co-directs the university's Centre for Economic History, and serves as the director of research impact for Queen's Management School. He obtained a PhD in Economic History from the London School of Economics and

Political Science in 2011. He researches topics and questions at the intersection of economic history and financial economics, cultural economics and demographic economics. He has published, among other places, in *The Journal of Economic History, Economic History Review* and *Explorations in Economic History*. Chris is an Associate of the Economics Network, an academic organisation supporting the teaching and learning of economics in universities in the UK. With Matthias Blum, he co-edited *An Economist's Guide to Economic History* (2018), a pedagogical resource aimed at introducing the field of economic history to economics students and their educators. He currently teaches a course called Communicating Economics to first-year undergraduate students on the BSc Economics degree pathway at Queen's University Belfast.

John Durant has spent his entire career in the broad field of public engagement with science and technology. In the 1990s, he was Assistant Director and Head of Science Communication at the Science Museum, London, where he led the creation of The Wellcome Wing, and before joining MIT, he was Executive Director of At-Bristol, a new science centre in the west of England. He is currently the Mark R. Epstein (Class of 1963) Director of the MIT Museum, an Adjunct Professor in the Science, Technology and Society Program at MIT, and a Faculty Dean at Pforzheimer House at Harvard University.

Eva Johnston is an experienced educator who specialises in the intersection of economics and history. As part of the Economic Education team, she creates classroom lessons, toolkits and activities that incorporate the wealth of primary and secondary source documents found in the St. Louis Fed's FRASER® digital library. Before joining the Federal Reserve Bank of St. Louis, she taught high school government, economics and history in the St. Louis area for 28 years.

Anna Killick explores both politicians' and voters' perceptions of the economy using qualitative methods. Her book *Politicians and Economic Experts: The Limits of Technocracy* will be published by Agenda in October 2022. It is based on work done by the Politics Department of University College London on a UKRI-funded project comparing mental models of the economy across five industrialised democracies. She has also used interviewing to explore voters' perceptions of the economy in a city on the south coast of England, in the book *Rigged: Understanding the Economy in Brexit Britain*. She is sections editor for the *Political Quarterly* journal.

Joan Leach is the Director of the Australian National Centre for Public Awareness of Science at the ANU. She has research and teaching interests in science communication, public engagement, policy, knowledge brokering, risk and ethics, and strives to make CPAS a home for inter- and transdisciplinary research and collaboration. Her work centres on theories of the public in science communication, language and rhetoric in science, and the challenge of ethics in science communication; at the moment, she has funded research projects on "commons" approaches in stem cell science, the use of synthetic biology for the future of agriculture and research to re-think responsible innovation in the Australian Context. She is most interested in sociological accounts of knowledge production and was editor of the journal *Social Epistemology* for nine years. Prof. Leach is also Chair of the National Committee for History and Philosophy of Science at the Australian Academy of Science.

Vicki Macknight works in the Centre for Science Communication at the University of Otago. Her work has been published in a range of journals including *Valuation Studies*, *Journal of Science Communication*, *Science as Culture* and *Social Epistemology*. She is the author of *Imagining Classrooms: Stories of Children, Teaching and Ethnography* (2016).

Jens Maesse is Senior Researcher (PD Dr habil.) at the Department of Sociology, University of Giessen (Germany). Jens' research focus is on discourse analysis, sociology of science and education, economic sociology and political economy. His publications include "Globalization strategies and the economics dispositive: Insights from Germany and the UK", *Historical Social Research* 43(3), 120–146 (2018) and "Translating Austerity: The formation and transformation of the EU economic constitution as discourse", *Interdisciplinary Political Studies*, 7(1), 61–94 (2021) (with Gerardo Costabile Nicoletta).

Carlo Martini is Associate Professor in Philosophy of Science at Vita-Salute San Raffaele University (Milan) and a visiting Adjunct Professor at the University of Helsinki. He has worked on the interface between science and policy, scientific expertise and science communication. His latest research focuses on the problem of pseudoscience and how it affects public trust in science. He is leader of the work package "Behavioral Tools for Building Trust" in the H2020 Project "Policy, Expertise and Trust" (https://peritia-trust.eu).

Deirdre Nansen McCloskey holds the Isaiah Berlin Chair in Liberal thought at the Cato Institute, Washington, and is Emerita Professor of Economics, History, English and Communication at the University of Illinois at Chicago. The author of two dozen books and editor of nine more, she has written some 500 scholarly and journalistic pieces in economics, economic history, rhetorical theory, philosophy of science, literary criticism, gender studies, theology, ethics, legal and political theory, and statistical theory and practice. Tenured in Economics at the University of Chicago in its glory days of the 1970s, she has taught and visited worldwide, as at Erasmus University of Rotterdam and the Institute for Advanced Study at Princeton. She is a fellow of the American Association for the Advancement of Science and of the American Academy of Arts and Sciences, and holds eleven honorary degrees. She is an active public intellectual, writing for US and foreign newspapers and magazines. Entering her ninth decade, Deo volente, she lives in a busy retirement from regular teaching in Chicago, travelling widely to keynote conferences and deliver lectures.

Fabien Medvecky is a senior lecturer in the Department of Science Communication at the University of Otago. Armed with graduate degrees in Philosophy and in Economics, he studies the relationship between knowledge and society, and how social interactions shape, create and direct what counts as knowledge. Dr Medvecky is especially interested in areas that are challenging and uncomfortable, from ethical and justice issues in communicating information to questions over contentious or controversial science and technologies (gene tech, alternative medicine, etc.). He also has a long-running interest in how economics (the discipline, not the economy) is made public and how that interacts with other forms of knowledge and expertise.

Stephan Pühringer is a socio-economist and Deputy Head of the Institute for Comprehensive Analysis of Economy (ICAE) at the University of Linz, Austria. Currently he is leading the interdisciplinary research project SPACE (www.spatial-competition.com), which is studying the performative impact of competition on the level of institutions, discourses and everyday practices. His research interests include competition research, political economy, history of economic thought, social studies of economics and neoliberalism studies. His recent publications include Pühringer, S.; Rath, J; Griesebner, T. (2021): *The Political Economy of Academic Publishing, PLoS ONE* 16(6): e0253226 and Kapeller, J.; Pühringer, S.; Grimm, C. (2021): "Paradigms and Policies: The Current State of Economics in the German-Speaking Countries", *Review of International Political Economy*, DOI: 10.1080/09692290.2021.1904269, online first.

The Rethinking Economics Team is an international network of students and recent graduates building a better economics for the classroom, with the support of academic allies. By organising campaigns, events and engaging projects, Rethinking Economics connects people globally to bring about economics education that is pluralist, realistic, diverse and decolonised.

Thierry Rossier is a visiting fellow at the Department of Sociology from the London School of Economics since Summer 2021, and a postdoctoral fellow at the Department of Management from the University of Fribourg since Summer 2022. Before that, he did a PhD at the University of Lausanne and was a guest research fellow at Copenhagen Business School. He has been funded by the Swiss National Science Foundation to work on elite coordination, and on gender inequalities within elite occupations and among business top managers. He is particularly interested in the social studies of economics, on the impact of economists in society and on the scientific and political distinctions among economists. He also works more generally on the social structuration of scientific disciplines and on scientific careers, networks and discourses. He specialises in the use of descriptive quantitative methods, such as geometric data analyses, social network analysis, sequence analysis or topic modelling. He recently published in the *British Journal of Sociology*, *Social Science Information* and *Global Networks*.

Thomas Shepherd is the Museum Director at the award-winning Economy Museum at the St. Louis Fed with more than 16 years of museum management experience. Shepherd managed the design and installation of the museum and its recent expansion, and currently oversees all the museum's operations. Prior to this role, Shepherd worked for eight years in various visitor experience management roles at the St. Louis Science Center.

Romesh Vaitilingam is an economics writer and communications consultant, the editor-in-chief of the *Economics Observatory* and a member of the editorial board of Vox. He is the author of numerous articles and several books in economics, finance, business and public policy, including *The Financial Times Guide to Using the Financial Pages*, now in its sixth edition (2011). As a specialist in translating economic and financial concepts into everyday language, Romesh has advised a number of government agencies and international institutions, including the European Central Bank, the European Bank for Reconstruction and Development and the UK's Department for International Development.

His work also involves consultancy for the economic research community, notably advising the European Economic Association, the Centre for Economic Performance at LSE and the Centre for Economic Policy Research on the management and development of their public profile; managing the IGM Forum surveys of economic experts; and training economists in communication skills. In 2003, he was awarded an MBE for services to economic and social science.

INTRODUCTION

Why Make Economics Public?

Vicki Macknight and Fabien Medvecky

Australia, 2011. The then Gillard government announced the forthcoming Clean Energy Act. This was essentially an emission trading scheme but was commonly referred to as the 'carbon tax' in Australia. The country entered a period of heated debate between various political factions – and in this setting, a particularly striking moment. Striking because nothing was said.

We are watching Q&A, a TV debate show, where a group of political and public figures respond to the audience's questions. The discussion turns to the Clean Energy Act, and in particular, how it should be implemented. One of the panellists claims that they would not tax individuals and they would only put the tax on producers because it shouldn't be everyday Aussies who pay for it. Economically, of course, this is an impossible claim.

Any student in ECON 101 would, or at least should, know that you can't choose who bears the burden of a tax based on whom you tax. The distribution of who pays a tax is determined by the elasticity of supply and demand. The *legal* tax incidence (who you tax) has little to no bearing on the *economic* tax incidence (who ends up bearing the additional cost).

What is so striking about this moment is that understanding the basics of tax distribution is fundamental to political, civic and economic participation. Yet no one on the panel picked up the misleading claim, no one in the audience picked it up and no one at home commented (the show had a running banner with viewers' texts and tweets at the bottom of the screen).

Now imagine a similar scenario, but one where a panellist claims that they would promote free antibiotics for the cold for everyone. They would almost certainly be corrected for failing to know the difference between bacterial and viral infections, either by their co-panellists and/or by the audience. The cold is most commonly a viral infection, and antibiotics won't do any good. Nearly

DOI: 10.4324/9781003283447-1

everyone knows that. I know that, and I have had neither a medical nor a science education. This is a measure of how successful the public understanding of science movement has been. Indeed, it is worth noting the fact that science has been made public so well while economics has not. There is no Economics Guy to match Bill Nye's the Science Guy.

Of course, there is plenty about the *economy* in the public sphere. Every newspaper has a section on the economy and often articles on finance too. But the economy is not economics. Economics is to the economy what science is to the natural world. The sciences are the disciplines that study, try to understand and find ways to interact with and manage the natural world. Likewise, economics is the discipline that studies, tries to understand and finds ways to interact with and manage economic interactions – including the economy. Understanding economics (the discipline) is essential to our capacity to engage in the economy in an informed way in much the same way understanding science is essential to our capacity to engage with the natural world in an informed way.

And so, we find ourselves faced with a situation like that in Australia, in 2011. The difference between legal versus economic tax incidence is as a fundamental distinction in economics as the bacterial versus viral infections distinction is in science. But no one corrected the false claim about taxes, even though taxes affect each and every one of us in such fundamental ways. That silence from politicians, experts and public alike said so much.

First, it highlighted the problem that economics is central to our personal, social and political life yet so distant and detached. As Keynes memorably said, "The ideas of economists and political philosophers, both when they are right and when they are wrong, are more powerful than is commonly understood. Indeed the world is ruled by little else" (Keynes, 1936, p. 383).

Economics impacts everyone. We notice this when staple goods are rising in price while reserve banks raise interest rates to try to put a lid on inflation. But it is also true in quieter times, any time we make decisions about how to spend our time, our money or our vote. In all these cases, people are using economic concepts like scarcity, opportunity cost, supply and demand or assessing the economic policy claims of politicians. This goes beyond budgeting or household management and into fundamental questions about what we value, our visions of the ideal world and our beliefs about why the real world falls short. In many cases, we might not realise we are using economics. We might even be using it badly. But this doesn't deny the importance of economic ideas in our lives. Bill Clinton underscored the role of economics in voting decisions and assessments of our everyday lives as he fought for re-election in the 1990s, "It's the economy, stupid".

Beyond its importance in the social and political sphere, economics also looms large as a valued academic subject, at least in the market place. PayScale and *Wall Street Journal*, in a 2007 study, assessed the mid-career (ten years post-graduation) incomes of various undergraduate majors (Needleman, 2008). The top four were various forms of engineering. The fifth was economics. Studying economics pays. It is valued as a degree and as a field in the currencies that matter – those of power and money.

Many people, though, are judged to be not very knowledgeable about economics. While methods of assessing economic knowledge are contentious (see Chapter 3), it is generally noted that many people, especially women, older people, and people with little money, tend to neither know economic terms nor feel confident with basic economic equations (see, for example, Lusardi and Mitchell, 2011, 2014; Walstad and Rebeck, 2002). Perhaps, this is not surprising; researchers have noted the gap between the beliefs of economists compared with everyday people. Sapienza and Zingales (2013) found that the more economists agreed between themselves, the more everyday people disagreed with them. Explanations of why this might tend to apply the words 'misunderstanding' and 'bias' to explain 'folk' beliefs about economics (see, for example, Boyer and Petersen, 2018; Kemp, 2007; Leiser and Shemesh, 2018). Not, one might think, the tone to take if you want people to listen to you. This, though, illustrates nicely the claim of Fourcade, Ollion and Algan (2015) that economists have a subjective sense of their own superiority, authority and entitlement.

So here's the challenge. Economics affects us all, in deep and multiple ways, both individually and collectively, yet it is largely dislocated from the public: kept technical and jargon-filled, hard to access and easy to misunderstand. If we are committed to a liberal ideal, a society where individuals can make informed decisions about their lives and can meaningfully engage in civic and political life, then we need to make economics significantly more public. Hence this book.

The good news is we don't need to reinvent the wheel, and this for two reasons. First, there are rich and well-developed fields that tackle the problem of how to make complex, often technical, expert knowledge more accessible and engaging to various publics; namely the public understanding of science and social studies of science movements. Since the Royal Society's 'The Public Understanding of Science' report nearly 40 years ago, there has been an explosion of interest in bringing science into the public domain. This work has been academic and practical, with a fast-growing academic field dedicated to studying efforts to make science public, and an ever-increasing set of practices and policies to increase engagement with, and understanding of, science and technology. Aims are not limited to communicating information about science and technology but also to engage society in challenging and democratically important questions from mRNA vaccines to GMO foods. With people working in museums, government agencies, educational settings and online to teach, advertise, engage, listen and discuss, there are tools aplenty.

Second, there are already some people, though too few, leading the charge in making economics public. A number of them have contributed to this volume.

This book then is a call to arms to bring the discipline of economics more into the public domain. And it has two aims. First, it makes a case for why we need to make economics public while exploring what, exactly, this might mean. Second, it suggests some ways that this can be done. Our authors provide both academic and practical tools for making economics public, from teaching economics students about communication to using interactive museums for engaging school students in fundamental concepts. Our authors are variously economists, philosophers, public understanding of science scholars, activists and communicators. Together they are beginning the hard work of building this exciting and emergent project – the public making of economics.

The book has four sections, loosely corresponding to *Why? How? Challenges* and *Economics and democracy*. Each section has its own introduction, outlining in brief how the chapters connect. At the end of each chapter, you will find some suggested further readings and some key questions which you can use to extend your thinking or as teaching aides.

The story we tell through these sections runs roughly as follows: First, economics is central to decision making in modern democracies, but little is done to bring knowledge of economics into the public sphere. This is startling when compared to science, a set of equally complex and technical disciplines important for decision making. This is Section One.

But, before readers become disheartened at the huge amount of work to be done, be assured that there are already committed people working in a range of ways to make economics more public. Online, in media, museums, networks, university classrooms and beyond, people are working to make economics more open, more inclusive and more committed to communication. This is our Section Two.

This, though, is challenging. Knowledge in the modern world is irreducibly complex, throwing up questions of authority, expertise, trust, morality, money and more. The question of how economics should see itself – the illusion that 'what is' can be separated in economic work from 'what should be' – ends Section Three.

Finally, we close the story with the grand and sweeping claim that economics and economies are inherently linked to political ideals, and these are always and indisputably matters of communication. A properly free polity is one that understands markets as being made up of words and deeds, underscored by a culture that embraces rich and sceptical conversations, about economics as well as other things.

That economics should be more public, why it isn't and how can we make it so, the challenges will we face, and the impact economics as communication has on the ways we see freedom – this is the story of the book.

To break this down further. In the first section, *why*, authors explain why economics is not more public. By contrasting the extensive efforts to make science more public, John Durant, the author of our first chapter, illuminates the importance of making more public the information and concepts central to decision making. He describes ways that science – a range of complex and technical subjects – has been made engaging and accessible to the public. He wonders about the role of economists' power for keeping the discipline closed. This provides a nice jumping-off spot for our next authors, Pierre Benz, Jens Maesse,

Stephan Pühringer and Thierry Rossier, to further break down the modes of that power and describe the ways the exciting and emergent field of Social Studies of Economics (SSE) has gone about studying the discipline. Anna Killick, the author of our third chapter, turns to one of the still poorly understood issues in the area – what do the public actually know about economics? She makes the argument that current knowledge of what the public know about economics is weak because of the ways the public have been asked. She suggests a new methodology, grasping both quantitative and qualitative data, and challenges us with a question too – who should have the power to say what economics the public should know?

In the second section, *how*, the authors describe the various ways they have been working to make economics more public to specific audiences and in specific places. First, we stand with Romesh Vaitilingam, a public-facing economist, who describes the ways he and his colleagues work between academia, policy makers and public. This is an inside look at the media- and online-savvy needed to do this work in the modern world. Next, with Thomas Shepherd and Eva Johnston, we visit the Economy Museum in St Louis, inspired by the Museo Interactivo de Economia in Mexico City. Here we grow to understand the challenge of how to make seemingly abstract economic concepts into exciting interactive displays for a range of audiences, including school-aged children. Next, we look with the Rethinking Economics team at the work that networks like theirs are doing to build a more diverse and inclusive discipline capable of having broader conversations between academics, policy makers, citizens and students. Finally, we think more about those students who may later be economists as Christopher L. Colvin describes the course he teaches to all first-year economics students at Queen's University Belfast. Economics is science, he teaches, but it is also literature, politics, history and philosophy, and underpinning it all, economics is communication.

The third section focusses on *challenges*, including complexity, politics, trust and ethics. This section starts with Vicki Macknight, who invites a reflection on the irreducible messiness of knowledge in an online environment. Next, Kevin Albertson argues that there is a paradox in democratic capitalism in that democracy, by inviting all to vote equally, is a left-wing innovation while capitalism, by promoting the right of private ownership, is a right-wing innovation. How to balance the rights of the many, including the right to knowledge, with the interests of the (increasingly rich and powerful) few? Carlo Martini considers the vexed question of how to tell the difference between high-quality, research-based economics and pseudo-economics, the swathes of more and less reliable work that might push policy makers and others in particular directions. Joan Leach and Fabien Medvecky turn to the ethics of communicating economics, in particular, the importance of recognising the sticky ground that we stand on when we try to separate positive and normative economics, or in other words, claims about what is from claims about what matters.

Deirdre Nansen McCloskey stands alone in a brief but grand Section Four, with her argument that economics and economies are always indisputably public

– and must remain so. This chapter calls on us to include even bigger ideas in our framing of economics. For McCloskey, an economic market is a rhetorical affair, one that requires a certain kind of liberty. This is a liberty to speak, discover, argue and persuade. "The economy", McCloskey argues, "does not work through capital. It works through discovery, of a better way. Thus free speech".

This book, then, is about how to make economics more public and the challenges we might face in the attempt. It is also, though, about why this is an important job, first for the concrete and pragmatic reasons of good personal and collective decision making, but second to reinforce the very under-girding of open and free societies.

References

Boyer, P., & Petersen, M. B. (2018). Folk-economic beliefs: An evolutionary cognitive model. *Behavioral and Brain Sciences, 41*, e158. doi:10.1017/S0140525X17001960.

Fourcade, M., Ollion, E., & Algan, Y. (2015). The superiority of economists. *Journal of Economic Perspectives, 29*(1), 89–114.

Kemp, S. (2007). Psychology and opposition to free trade. *World Trade Review, 6*(1), 25–44. doi:10.1017/S147475606003089.

Keynes, J. M. (1936). *The General Theory of Employment, Interest and Money*. London: Macmillan.

Leiser, D., & Shemesh, Y. (2018). *How We Misunderstand Economics and Why It Matters: The Psychology of Bias, Distortion and Conspiracy*. Routledge. doi:10.4324/9781315675343.

Lusardi, A., & Mitchell, O. S. (2011). Financial literacy around the world: an overview. *Journal of Pension Economics & Finance, 10*(4), 497–508.

Lusardi, A., & Mitchell, O. S. (2014). The economic importance of financial literacy: Theory and evidence. *Journal of Economic Literature, 52*(1), 5–44.

Needleman, S. E. (31 July, 2008). Ivy Leaguers' Big Edge: Starting Pay. *The Wall Street Journal*.

Sapienza, P., & Zingales, L. (2013). Economic experts versus average Americans. *American Economic Review, 103*(3), 636–642.

Walstad, W. B., & Rebeck, K. (2002). Assessing the economic knowledge and economic opinions of adults. *The Quarterly Review of Economics and Finance, 42*(5), 921–935.

SECTION ONE

Why Should We Make Economics More Public?

This first section introduces themes that run through the book. Though written by authors from very different disciplinary places, and focussing on different motivations, all agree on the need for knowledge of economics to be considered a public good.

Who gets a voice? Who gets to say what knowledge is necessary? Knowledge for what purpose? These are some of the questions our first authors bring.

We start with Durant, a foundational scholar of the Public Understanding of Science movement (part of the social studies of science field that has been active for decades now) who offers clarity by way of comparison. What makes science and economics different such that knowledge of one is treated as a public right and the other not?

We then move to Benz et al. who are interested in the emergent discipline of the Social Studies of Economics and who outline the various lines of enquiry of that discipline. The interest of scholars working in this area ranges from the relationships between individuals to institutions, social structures, networks and discourses, though in all cases, they seek to understand how power is distributed – shared, kept latent and hoarded.

Finally, we move to Killick who has studied what people know about economics – and how academics know what people know. She outlines how researchers have gone about assessing public knowledge of economics: first by testing levels of knowledge against a pre-assumed standard or by investigating in deeper and more qualitative ways what people do know about economics. She argues for a third way that synthesises the strengths of these two approaches. She closes by wondering how we might come to decide what knowledge is important for the public to hold – and indeed, who 'we' even is.

DOI: 10.4324/9781003283447-2

Together, these chapters make it clear that economics can't and shouldn't be separated from the public forum. But while economics and communication are inseparable, *who* gets to have a voice and *who* is listened to is very much a matter of power.

1

TOWARDS A POLITICAL ECONOMY OF PUBLIC UNDERSTANDING OF ECONOMICS

John Durant

There are many ways to study something, but one of the best is by contrast. Do you want to know what makes the earth special? Try contrasting it with other planets. Would you like to know what makes a country special? Try comparing it with its neighbours. Are you curious about what makes a person special? Try finding out how they differ from those around them.

On and off, I've been involved with public understanding of science for more than 40 years. During this long period, I've often wondered what makes science special. Why have I devoted so much effort to probing science, prodding science and problematizing science in the public domain? From a time before public understanding of science was even a recognized thing, I've been concerned with the place of science in people's lives. And now, after many years of conceptualization and re-conceptualization of putting up labels like "public understanding of science" and then tearing them down again, in favour of "public engagement with science" or some other moniker, I still find myself happily and – hopefully – productively employed in the same place.

And I am not alone. Over the course of the last half-century, and around the globe, there has been a virtual avalanche of seminars, conferences, research papers, magazine articles, books, radio and TV programmes, films and (more recently) social media initiatives, alongside a multi-billion-dollar industry of practical activities – science museums, science centres, science festivals and the like – all devoted to one aspect or another of the thing that is still sometimes referred to as public understanding of science. Why? Why all this fuss? What is it about science that keeps so many science communicators busy, gets some scientists queuing up for communication training and has a fairly large number of funding agencies reaching for their proverbial check books?

DOI: 10.4324/9781003283447-3

Occasionally, scholars have looked at these questions head-on. They have wondered, for example, whether the preoccupation with the relationship between science and the public is an expression of some kind of professional neurosis within science itself. As Brian Wynne once asked, are we dealing here with "new horizons", or merely "a hall of mirrors"?[1] (Wynne, 1992a, pp. 37–43). But this is not the approach that I intend to take here, in a volume about something that wants to be called public understanding of economics. I say that it wants to be called this because to date, there has not really been anything comparable to public understanding of science in relation to any other academic disciplines. There really is not, for example, a well-funded global movement for the public understanding of, say, history (there should be!), literature (yes!) or – turning at last to the point at hand – economics.

It is important not to overstate things here. There are, indeed, literatures on "economic literacy" and economics education, and these bear at least some similarities to the literatures on "science literacy" and science education. Additionally, concern about public understanding of economics has been expressed in a number of special initiatives. In the UK, for example – which, as in the case of public understanding of science, appears to have taken something of a lead here – the Royal Society of Arts and Manufactures recently commissioned a "Citizens' Economic Council", in order to "[prototype] a range of democratic innovations on economic policy" and "to be a catalyst for sparking a broader public discussion about the goals and priorities of economic policy" (Patel et al., 2018). And, again in the UK, the Economic Statistics Centre of Excellence, a collaboration with the Office of National Statistics, issued a report on public understanding of economics and economic statistics (Runge and Hudson, 2020).

It is true, then, that some effort has been expended on public understanding of economics; but, to be frank, this effort is dwarfed by what has been going on in public understanding of science. On 21 March 2021, I searched Google Scholar for publications on "public understanding of science" and pulled up 49,400 links. A similar search for publications on "public understanding of economics" yielded just 104 links. A related but different comparison is provided in Figure 1.1, which displays a Google Ngram of the relative numbers of Google Books about "public understanding of science" and "public understanding of economics".

At the very least, this graph displays a striking contrast, and it is this contrast that I shall explore here.[2] We may start by noting that the size and scale of the contrast are somewhat surprising. Superficially, we might have expected public understanding of economics to rise in prominence along with, or even as part of, the public understanding of science. Like science, after all, economics has everyday, real-world relevance. Like science, again, economics is phenomenally complex and typically requires a great deal of training in order to be properly understood – so it would appear to need an effort in the domain of public understanding. And of course, economics is arguably a science itself; or at least, it is often taken as such. It will be worth reflecting briefly on each of these points.

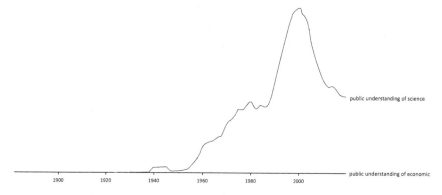

FIGURE 1.1   Google Books Ngram Viewer (public understanding of science; public understanding of economics).

Source: Google Ngram Viewer (2021).

First is the question of real-world relevance. From the very beginning, and consistently up to the present, advocates of the public understanding of science have claimed that one reason for the importance of their subject is its practical, real-world relevance. Science, as it is argued, permeates our culture and has multiple everyday applications and implications. In the era of Covid-19, it may seem unnecessary to labour this point. But far beyond public health, science has obvious everyday impacts: at home (e.g., energy supply, new materials); at work (e.g., computers and computing); and at play (e.g., inter-continental travel and tourism and the burgeoning videogame industry). Know it or not, and like it or not, science touches all our lives virtually all the time.

And yet, of course, exactly the same thing is true of economics. The creation and distribution of wealth is an unavoidable aspect of human existence; indeed, it is, perhaps, the single greatest preoccupation of the political process. Except in the most extreme cases (what would these even be – the lives of hermits, perhaps?), a person cannot exist without being economically active; and the question of what kind of economic activity to undertake dominates career decisions and working lives. This, surely, is why economic affairs loom so large in public media: in daily financial and business reports; in regular phone-ins and self-help programmes; and in countless discussions devoted to current affairs. With all of this media coverage, one might expect to find a public understanding of economics movement of some kind. And yet, with just a few honourable exceptions, as we've seen, such a movement hardly exists – hence, arguably, the need for this book.

Now to the second of our comparisons between economics and science: complexity. Almost legendarily, science is complicated and difficult. It is abstract, frequently mathematical, and inclined to the use of highly specialized vocabularies that are not widely understood outside their special fields of application. So much, I suppose, is obvious. But, equally obviously, all these points apply in full measure to economics. In 2018, *USA Today* reported that as many as 33% of Americans filed their own taxes each year (Smith, 2018); but, by the same token, this meant that two-thirds of Americans did not. Presumably, this sizeable majority depended on accountants to help them with the task of completing their tax returns – because they're so complicated. And of course, personal taxation is just the tip of the economic iceberg. If anybody thinks that quantum mechanics or organic chemistry is uniquely complex, let them try their hands at economic game theory, or agent-based computational economics, or mathematical modelling of hedge fund performance. As the distinguished MIT economist, Nobel Laureate Robert Solow, once put it rather quaintly: "Economics is no longer a fit conversation piece for ladies and gentlemen. It has become a technical subject" (Solow, 1988). Which being the case, we may ask: why such relative inattention to public understanding of economics?

Third and last, we turn to the vexed question: is economics itself a science? This is the subject of much debate, and – let it be said – not a little jocularity, mainly on the part of people far outside the world of economics. One wisecrack has it that anything that calls itself a science isn't. Thus, on the one side, we are invited to consider ostensibly "real" sciences such as physics, chemistry, and biology, which don't bother to call themselves out; while on the other side, we are to be amused by subjects like economic science, political science, and – an extreme case, admittedly – domestic science, which proudly adopt the scientific moniker. It's easy to see that there is some academic fun to be had here; but in truth, this is a pretty feeble joke, and it doesn't actually work well, even on its own terms. Leaving aside the social sciences, what are we to make, for example, of materials science, brain science (and its close cousin, neuroscience), or computer science? The root meaning of the word science is simply knowledge (*scientia*). At the very least, it will require a complex historical argument – itself, we should note, of questionable scientific status – to show how one subset of organized bodies of knowledge has come to claim privileged scientific status, in contrast to all the others. There is not much enlightenment to be had for our purposes here.

We're left, then, with the puzzling contrast: why has so much attention been lavished on public understanding of science, while so little has been given to public understanding of economics? This puzzle gives us reason to think again about why particular subjects become targets for concern about public understanding. Let us look, then, at some of the other arguments that have been used to justify concern with public understanding of science. One of these, as already noted, is practical, but another is essentially political. The key point of the political argument is the claim that science is bound up in many public policy questions so that the argument for public understanding of science becomes part of a larger argument about the importance of having an educated citizenry capable of making informed judgements about politically important issues. If we want illustrations, once again we are faced with a rather wide choice: energy policy, health policy, and defence policy all provide multiple examples.

Once again, though, the political argument doesn't appear to cleave helpfully between science and economics. If science is relevant to public policy-making, how much more relevant is economics! Think, for example, of fiscal policy, industrial policy, trade policy, or employment policy: all appear to require a close familiarity with economics. If there is a reason for the relative lack of apparent concern with public understanding of economics, it cannot be because economics is perceived to be of no consequence in the public square. And coincidentally, we have already seen that this is not the case, by noting how commonplace is public discussion of economic issues in the media. If anyone doubts the perceived public importance of economics in comparison with science, let them count the number of column inches (or minutes of broadcast time) devoted to these two distinct areas in, say, *The New York Times*, or the *London Times*, or on CNN or Fox News. By any of these measures, there is no shortage of public interest in economics.

This brings us to the need to consider a third argument for public understanding of science, which may be more promising. In addition to the practical and the political arguments, there have always been a number of, what I shall call, scientific arguments for public understanding of science. By describing an argument as scientific in this context, I mean, simply that, it claims that the health of science itself, as an endeavour, depends in some way on public understanding. One scientific argument points out that much scientific research depends on public funding and that the provision of such funding may be contingent on a measure of public support for science. A second argument, sometimes referred to as the "pipeline argument", suggests that the supply of sufficient numbers of well-qualified young people wishing to become scientists may depend on cultivation of interest in science among young people. And so on.

It is unquestionably true that much scientific research depends on public funding. In the U.S. alone, the National Science Foundation (NSF), the National Institutes of Health, and other federal agencies typically allocate several billion dollars each year for civic scientific research; and beyond this, even larger sums are spent by the Defence Department on military research and development, at least some parts of which are allocated to things that can properly be described as scientific. One measure of the perceived importance of this issue of public funding in the U.S. is that trends in public expenditure on science are routinely used by the NSF as part of its annual "Science Indicators" report on the state of health of the body scientific (National Science Board, 2020). Today, in the U.S., there are lobbying organizations that exist specifically to build public support for science funding (see, for example, Research America, 2023). Looking across the Atlantic for a moment, I can also say that few of us who were involved in these issues in the UK in the early 1980s thought that the crisis in public expenditure on science at that time was entirely unrelated to the parallel rise of the public understanding of science movement.

The "pipeline" argument is harder to evaluate. Certainly, many scientists are inclined to think that the future of their subjects is imperilled by a potential lack of supply of talented young entrants to the field; and I have found that the same perception exists widely among engineers. Whether these perceptions are accurate is, however, quite another question. In fact, there is a fairly large literature (much of it econometric!) on the extent to which there have been shortages in the labour market for trainee scientists and engineers at various times and in various places. (The literature is large, but see, for example, Smith and Gorard, 2011; Bracey, 2008; Butz et al., 2003.) As I read in this literature, a short summary verdict is as follows: the situation is complex and unclear; but the case for a pipeline crisis is very much less clear-cut than many scientists have been inclined to believe. I suspect that a shortage of plumbers in many western economies in recent decades is much easier to document – not least, from relevant labour rates – than is a shortage of physicists, chemists, biologists, or whatever. However, this is arguably not quite to the point. If scientists and/or engineers *think* that their subjects are imperilled by labour shortages, this may influence their attitudes towards public outreach, and whether they are objectively correct in their views. In this special sense, at least, I am inclined to think that the pipeline argument has been a significant issue in the rise of the modern public understanding of science movement.

Here, at last, we may have found a difference between science and economics that is relevant to our contrast. Science often feels itself vulnerable to the winds of public sentiment and public support. But what if this is not really true, or any rate not true to anything like the same extent, in the case of economics? What if economists on the whole feel quite secure in the modern world? In this case, we might expect that, on the average, economists might be less sensitive to and/or concerned about the relationship between their discipline and the wider public, and by the same token, we might expect them to be less inclined to invest time and effort in public outreach. In a situation like this, there would likely be less of a "push", as it were, from within the field of economics, encouraging it to be more open and responsive to the wider community.

What follows is speculative; but here is what I suspect is going on. I think that economics may be positioned in the public sphere in ways that are very different from the positioning of most sciences. First, economics may be less dependent on the contingencies of public funding for its ongoing research – presumably, because it obtains a greater proportion of that funding from commercial and other private sources. Second, there may be no perceived shortage of young economists, rising to fill the ranks of the profession in the years ahead. Anecdotally, I know from the experience of living in a residential community of undergraduates, that economics is currently one of the most popular undergraduate subjects (along with computer science, as it happens). Presumably, this is because many families see an academic training in economics as a sure path to a successful career. Another anecdote that points in this same direction is that, in recent years, there has been something of a "brain drain", from highly mathematical sciences such as physics, into high finance, to which some talented theoreticians have been attracted by the far higher incomes that are available there (see, for example, Weatherall, 2013).

There is at least some research that is consonant with these speculations. In an extremely interesting web-based survey study conducted in the U.S. in 2014, Medvecky and Macknight canvassed opinions on the relative importance of science and economics to the solution of major societal challenges. Somewhat to their surprise, the authors found that most respondents viewed science as being far more important than economics to the solution of such challenges. The differences were quite large, and they were statistically significant. In considering various explanations for these results, the authors wrote:

> Perhaps the reason people see science as more important than economics in solving our societal challenges is not because it really is any better, and nor is it because economics is so dismal; maybe it is because science has been over-sold (or economics under-sold).
>
> *(Medvecky and Macknight, 2015)*

This is a single survey study, with all the limitations that go along with that. However, the study is at least suggestive; and, if nothing else, it indicates the need for further study to see how far the self-promotion of different academic disciplines in the public sphere may have helped shape public attitudes towards them. Consistent with the findings of Medvecky and Macknight, I suggest that public understanding of science has been driven by a felt need within the scientific community to persuade the public of the relevance of science to major societal challenges. By contrast, it would appear that economists in the English-speaking world have not experienced such a felt need in recent decades – or at least, they have not experienced it to anything like the same extent. Public understanding initiatives should be understood as contingent upon the larger structural relationship(s) that individual disciplines have with the societies in which they are embedded. If further investigation supports this notion, then we shall be faced with the irony that, in the end, economic factors may have contributed to the rather slow growth to date in the public understanding of economics.

Digging Deeper

Discussion Questions

1. How do you know about science?
2. How do you know about economics?
3. Why is it important to know about science? What about economics?

Suggested Further Reading

Durant, J. R., Evans, G. A., & Thomas, G. P. (1989). The public understanding of science. *Nature, 340*(6228), 11–14.

Notes

1 Wynne kept up what is probably the single most incisive and sustained critique of the public understanding movement through the 1980s and beyond. See, for example: Wynne (1992b), Wynne (1993), Wynne (2003), Millar and Wynne (1988), and Irwin and Wynne (1996).
2 Note that the graph also suggests that "public understanding of science" has waxed and waned over time. The popularity of the term peaked in the last two decades of the twentieth century, and then it began to decline. This is not, I think, for lack of interest or attention, but rather because of a growing preference for alternative monikers such as public engagement with science.

References

Bracey, G. W. (2008). On the shortage of scientists and engineers. *Phi Delta Kappan*, *89*(7), 536–538.

Butz, W. P., Bloom, G. A., Gross, M. E., Kelly, T. K., Kofner, A., & Rippen, H. E. (2003). Isthere a shortage of scientists and engineers? How would we know. *Santa Monica, Calif.: RAND Corporation, IP-241-OSTP*. Available online at: https://europepmc.org/books/n/nap10727/a2000882addd00165/?extid=20669479&src=med&fid=a2000882addd00168.

Google Ngram Viewer (2021). Books.google.com. Available online at: https://books.google.com/ngrams/graph?content=public+understanding+of+science%2Cpublic+understanding+of+economics&year_start=1920&year_end=2019&corpus Accessed 20/3/2021.

Irwin, A., & Wynne, B, eds. (1996). *Misunderstanding science? The public reconstruction of science and technology*. Cambridge & New York: Cambridge University Press.

Medvecky, F., & Macknight, V. (2015). Who can solve our biggest challenges? Perceptions of the relative importance of science and economics. *Perceptions of the Relative Importance of Science and Economics (August 25, 2015)*. Available at SSRN: https://ssrn.com/abstract=2650925 or http://dx.doi.org/10.2139/ssrn.2650925.

Millar, R., & Wynne, B. (1988). Public understanding of science: from contents to processes. *International Journal of Science Education*, *10*(4), 388–398.

National Science Board (2020). The State of U.S. Science and Engineering 2020. *Science and Engineering Indicators*, Alexandria, Virginia. Available online at: https://ncses.nsf.gov/pubs/nsb20201.

Patel, R., Gibbon, K., & Greenham, T. (2018). Building a public culture of economics. Report of the RSA Citizens' Economic Council, Royal Society of Arts, London, 2018.

Research America (2023). Available online at: https://www.researchamerica.org/.

Runge, J., & Hudson, N. (2020). Public understanding of economics and economic statistics. *EScoE Occasional Paper*, 3.

Smith, E., & Gorard, S. (2011). Is there a shortage of scientists? A re-analysis of supply for the UK. *British Journal of Educational Studies*, *59*(2), 159–177.

Smith, J. (2018, February 3). Tax season: 10 tips for doing your taxes yourself. *USA Today*. https://www.usatoday.com/story/money/taxes/2018/02/03/tax-season-10-tips-doing-your-taxes-yourself/1020645001/.

Solow, R. M. (1988, March 20). The wide, wide world of wealth. *New York Times*. See: https://www.nytimes.com/1988/03/20/books/the-wide-wide-world-of-wealth.html?scp=1.

Weatherall, J. O. (2013). *The physics of wall street: a brief history of predicting the unpredictable*. New York: Houghton Mifflin Harcourt.

Wynne, B. (1992a). Public understanding of science research: new horizons or hall of mirrors? *Public Understanding of Science*, *1*(1), 37.

Wynne, B. (1992b). Misunderstood misunderstanding: social identities and public uptake of science. *Public Understanding of Science*, *1*(3), 281.

Wynne, B. (1993). Public uptake of science: a case for institutional reflexivity. *Public Understanding of Science*, *2*(4), 321.

Wynne, B. (1996 [2003]). May the sheep safely graze? D. Pepper, F. Webster, & G. Revill (Eds.), *Environmentalism: critical concepts*, Vol. IV. New York: Routledge, pp. 186–226.

2

POWER AND ECONOMICS[1]

Pierre Benz, Jens Maesse, Stephan Pühringer and Thierry Rossier

Economics as a Source and a Product of Power

During the last decades, economics has gained influence and power in many countries and several social contexts. "Economists are everywhere", stated Marion Fourcade (2009: 1), in a widely received book that remains very influential in the field of research of the Social Studies of Economics (SSE). Nearly 15 years later, this observation is far from being outdated. The Covid-19 crisis has made particularly visible the outstanding authority given to economists and their discourse, which are omnipresent in the media and political sphere. They participated in task forces and have influenced decisions from supporting measures to environmental and public health policies. Overall, the channels through which economists influence the economic, political and social spheres are widespread: they occupy an important position in private firms and governmental bodies, act as advisors and are very active in public discourses. Yet, the relationship between power and knowledge production is a complex phenomenon that crucially accounts for the special role of economics in contemporary societies.

Economics is not only a source of power but also a product of power and domination. Indeed, economics as an academic discipline and a profession alike remains heterogeneous and subject to constant theoretical and methodological struggles that define the boundaries of the discipline. The interaction between power and knowledge is complex and consequently cannot be defined without carefully studying both the power struggles that exist within the profession and the overall influence economics exerts in many spheres of society. Both internal and external dynamics impact economic sciences, which is understood as the main source of economic knowledge. Accordingly, one should conceive economics first as an arena in which researchers compete for the validity of their research results, rather than as a unified scientific community.

DOI: 10.4324/9781003283447-4

Against this backdrop, the SSE has developed as a field for the analysis of the role of economists in society. The purpose of SSE is precisely to study the interactions between individuals, social structures, networks and discourses to uncover what makes the nature and the form of power and economics so complex. Following the path-breaking works of Coats (1993), Fourcade (2009), Hall (1989), Lebaron (2001), Mirowski (1991) and Morgan (1990), a huge array of young scholars have sought to develop a field of research out of the canonical classics (Aistleitner et al., 2018; Hirschman & Pop Berman, 2014; Maesse et al., 2017, 2021b; Mata & Medema, 2013; Montecinos & Markoff, 2009; Schmidt-Wellenburg & Lebaron, 2018a). This chapter offers an overview of three analytical dimensions that fit in the analytical framework of SSE: discourse analysis, performativity studies and governmentality studies; network studies; and field analysis. Such a methodological and conceptual apparatus is designed to underline the complex relationship between power and economics, especially the various ways through which economists can display their influence on society. This approach includes several challenges that need to be analysed from a critical and interdisciplinary perspective. Furthermore, it offers insights into recent trajectories of the formation and consolidation of the recently evolving field of SSE.

Everywhere But Not Everyone

One of the very strengths of economists is their ability to be omnipresent across different policy fields, administrations, lobby groups, think tanks, union firms, banks and other organisations. Indeed, the list of positions held by economists is particularly long and diverse and often reaches the (very) top of the institutional hierarchies of different sectors in society. The nature of their functions is also multiple and ranges from consulting and expert to executive positions. At the international level, economists work in influential organisations such as the IMF, the World Bank, the WTO and the European Central Bank. They are also regularly called upon to perform as consultants or advisors in diverse policy fields from fiscal to health and social security. They are very present in the media sphere, which provides them with a platform to influence public discourses. Moreover, as part of consulting teams, they can act as economic experts and translate their symbolic capital into policy by coining core "economic imaginaries". In general terms, economists have become a very dominant professional group that distinguishes them from traditional professions.

Whereas the scope of their activities is overall extremely diverse, influence is unequally distributed among economists and subject to strong hierarchies. Economists are endowed with various volume and types of resources and the stratification of the profession has some far-reaching implications for the discipline. While some economists are powerful political, corporate or media actors invested at the local or national levels, others have a large scientific or expertise influence and are strongly embedded within transnational academic networks. Consequently, the analysis of power and economics must take into account the multiple channels of influence of economists in different spheres of power together with the power mechanisms that structure the profession. Aside from the previously mentioned analysis of power through the positions held, there is also a strain of research that focuses on the political power of economic ideas, the performativity of economic models and the role of economists as "public intellectuals". Here, scholars focus on several indirect channels of influence, which often are mediated by intermediaries such as think tanks or media outlets. The core section of this chapter exposes three different analytical views on power and economics. First, it develops the role of economic expert discourses as power devices for the formation of influential expertise. It also investigates the concept of governmentality to analyse the production of power and knowledge between science and society. Second, it focuses on economists' networks between academia, politics and the media. Third, it develops the interest to consider economics as a social field to investigate the issues of legitimacy and the internal stratification of the profession.

Three Analytical Views on Power and Economics

If we follow the classical study by Dahl (1961), who defines power as the actual ability to make (political) decisions, we would state that the power of economists only consists in such a material ability. However, this very narrow definition ignores two very important sources of power. First, power does not need to be used to exist and, in this sense, position alone confers power (Mills, 2000 [1956]). Second, power does not have to be material, it also resides in discourses and various mechanisms of micro-power (Foucault, 2008). Because knowledge is power, it is necessary to understand how knowledge is produced and subsequently spread.

A first analytical view of power calls for the study of economic expert knowledge, mainly from three perspectives. Economic historians and cultural sociologists mostly study paradigms, as well as hegemonic or marginalised forms of knowledge to understand the influence of power relations on the production of economic truths (Coats, 1993; Morgan, 1990; Dobusch & Kapeller, 2009; Mirowski, 1991; Ötsch et al., 2017). Following these studies, the influence of economic expert knowledge on society has gained major importance as a research area. In this framework, performativity studies have shown how economics as a form of discourse impacts the formation of markets and firms (Callon, 1998; MacKenzie et al., 2007), while other studies rather focus on the formation of legitimacy, argumentation strategies and speaker positions by economic expert discourses (Fitzgerald & O'Rourke, 2015; Maesse, 2015; Pühringer & Griesser, 2020). The forms of circulation of knowledge as well as the various types of interpretative adoption by experts, professionals, politicians and media are central issues for these approaches, which consider economic expertise as a means of exercising power in different social contexts (Schmidt-Wellenburg, 2018). The third form of discourse analytical perspective focuses on informal social rules in organisations, the tacit knowledge in professional fields and the informal knowledge that is needed to control access to certain institutions and power positions

(Maesse, 2018; Rossier & Bühlmann, 2018). This approach of economics and economic expertise as a form of "soft power" is deepened even further by scholarship focusing on Foucault's ground-breaking concepts of governmentality and neoliberalisation (Dean, 1999; Foucault, 2008; Miller, 2001). The economy is approached through the production of subjectivities, that is the role neoliberal ideologies and economic theories play in the production of political perceptions and interpretative frames (Zuidhof, 2012). This analysis of the governmentality of neoliberalism can be applied to various contexts, and the main contribution of governmentality approaches can be seen in their ability to connect a critical view of knowledge in relation to new approaches to power and domination, especially when analysing how discourses underpinning neoliberalism are embodied in identities and subjectivities (Gill & Scharff, 2011) and materialise in everyday life (Afsary, 2021).

The second analytical view, which focuses on relationships between individuals as sources of power, analyses network structures in economics. It investigates the role of interpersonal relations in the transmission of economic knowledge into politics but also within academic economics. A social network perspective enables to highlight the connections of economists to powerful elites and their involvement in policy-making processes or in the general spreading of economic ideas (Mirowski & Plehwe, 2009; Salas-Porras & Murray, 2017). Both personal networks (e.g. co-authorships, collaborations) and institutional networks (e.g. memberships, positions) are analysed to highlight the role of such networks in the transmission of economic knowledge into policy-making (Pühringer, 2020; Flickenschild & Afonso, 2019; Kapeller et al., 2021). When focusing on intra-academic networks, researchers are typically interested in analysing stratification logics that lead to hierarchies inside academia. In this regard, social network analysis is often combined with bibliometric and/or biographical analyses (Coman, 2019; Beyer & Pühringer, 2021). Recent studies for example investigate "citation cartels" between economic journals and authors (Önder & Treviö, 2015) or, on a more individual level, the crucial role of academic networks in shaping prospects for successful academic careers (Bühlmann et al., 2018; Rossier, 2020). Thus, network analytical approaches contribute to the debate on the public and political impact of economics by providing novel empirical analyses of social networks of economists inside as well as outside academia.

The third approach on power and economics focuses on the mechanisms of power and domination which are induced by inequalities inherent to social structures. These studies rely on the key concept of *field* (Bourdieu, 2005) to analyse the "objective" relations between individuals' social positions. In this perspective, economists are seen as competing to define what is sound economics (Lebaron, 2000). In this struggle, not everyone has the same legitimacy to speak out and the individuals who decide are those who hold the most resources among those considered decisive. The distribution of these resources is involved in systemic processes allowing their garnering by those who possess them (Savage et al., 2005). The hierarchy in the volume and type of resources owned defines the stratification of positions within the profession, and the scientific and political position-takings of individuals (Lebaron, 2001). In other words, power here does not (only) come from discourses' performativity nor interpersonal networks, but by the possession of specific resources (e.g. financial or knowledge resources), which confer power because they are unequally distributed. This is also true beyond the economic sphere such as in academia, where financial resources play an increasingly important role (Braun, 2001; Benz et al., 2021). A few US departments and the "Nobel Prize", which shape academic careers and citations (Korom, 2020), and the import of resources acquired in those departments, provide economists with advantageous positions in their home country (Dezalay & Garth, 2002; Gautier Morin & Rossier, 2021). This analysis of the resources held by economists is all the more interesting as they occupy a very important place in the field of power, that is, the field of the dominant individuals from all the other fields (Bourdieu, 1996). Powerful economists, therefore, contribute to spread an "economic belief", which tend, to reflect the interests of an elite capitalist class (Gerth & Mills, 1953).

Conclusion

Economists are not just a social group with increasing power over time, they certainly are to be considered as the producers of some of the most important tools and perceptions that govern today's societies (Schmidt-Wellenburg & Lebaron, 2018b). Their impressive influence from policy-making to individual behaviours is rooted as much in their positions among the public administration and private sector elites (Rossier et al., 2017, Klüger, 2018) as in their discourses that have an influence well beyond the profession's borders, up to the political arena (Schmidt-Wellenburg, 2018) or the media (Gautier Morin, 2019). This contribution has sought to show different ways of analysing the links between power and economics, focusing on three main analytical axes: discourses, performativity and governmentality; networks; and "objective" social relations determined by the unequal distribution of power resources in the social structure.

Digging Deeper

Discussion Questions

1. Where do economists work?
2. How important is economics to decision makers and the voting public?
3. How powerful are economists in influencing decision makers and the voting public?

Suggested Further Reading

Fourcade, M., Ollion, E., & Algan, Y. (2015). The superiority of economists. *Journal of Economic Perspectives*, 29(1), 89–114.

Note

1 This chapter is an adapted version of Maesse et al. (2021a).

References

Afsary, A. (2021). De la contraception hormonale à la contraception « naturelle » : Post-féminisme et transformation du rapport à soi. In F. Balard, & I. Voléry (Eds.), *La médicalisation des âges en France*. Nancy: Presses universitaires de Nancy, 25-44.

Aistleitner, M., Kapeller, J., & Steinerberger, S. (2018). The Power of Scientometrics and the Development of Economics. *Journal of Economic Issues*, 52(3), 816–834.

Benz, P., Bühlmann, F., & Mach, A. (2021). The Transformation of Professors' Careers: Standardization, Hybridization, and Acceleration? *Higher Education*, 81(5), 967–985.

Beyer, K., & Pühringer, S. (2021). Divided We Stand? Professional Consensus and Political Conflict in Academic Economics. ICAE Working Paper Series (94).

Bourdieu, P. (1996). *The State Nobility: Elite Schools in the Field of Power*. Cambridge: Polity Press; Oxford: Blackwell Publishers Ltd.

Bourdieu, P. (2005). *The Social Structures of the Economy*. Cambridge: Polity Press.

Braun, D. (2001). Regierungsmodelle und Machtstrukturen an Universitäten. In E. Stölting, & U. Schimank (Eds.), *Die Krise der Universitäten* (pp. 243–263). Wiesbaden: Westdeutscher Verlag.

Bühlmann, F., Rossier, T., & Benz, P. (2018). The Elite Placement Power of Professors of Law and Economic Sciences. In O. Korsnes, J. Hjellbrekke, M. Savage, J. Heilbron, & F. Bühlmann (Eds.), *New Directions in Elite Studies*. London: Routledge (Taylor & Francis).

Callon, M. (Ed.). (1998). *The Laws of the Markets*. Oxford: Blackwell.

Coats, A. B. (1993). *The Sociology and Professionalization of Economics: British and American Economic Essays* (Vol. 2). Abingdon-on-Thames: Routledge.

Coman, R. (2019). Transnational Economists in the Eurozone Crisis: Professional Structures, Networks and Ideas. *New Political Economy*, 93(3), 1–14.

Dahl, R. (1961). *Who Governs? Democracy and Power in an American City*. New Haven, CT: Yale University Press.

Dean, M. (1999). *Governmentality: Power and Rule in Modern Society*. Thousand Oaks, CA: Sage.

Dezalay, Y., & Garth, B. (2002). *The Internationalization of Palace Wars: Lawyers, Economists, and the Contest to Transform Latin American States*. Chicago, IL: Chicago University Press.

Dobusch, L., & Kapeller, J. (2009). Why Is Economics Not an Evolutionary Science? New Answers to Veblen's Old Question. *Journal of Economic Issues*, 43(4), 867–898.

Fitzgerald, J., & O'Rourke, B. K. (2015). Performing Economics: How Economics Discourse Gets Enacted in Radio News Interviews. *10th International Conference in Interpretive Policy Analysis,* Dublin: Technological University.

Flickenschild, M., & Afonso, A. (2019). Networks of Economic Policy Expertise in Germany and the United States in the Wake of the Great Recession. *Journal of European Public Policy*, 26(9), 1292–1311.

Foucault, M. (2008). *The Birth of Biopolitics. Lectures at the Collège de France, 1978–1979*. London: Palgrave Macmillan.

Fourcade, M. (2009). *Economists and Societies: Discipline and Profession in the United States, Britain, and France, 1890s to 1990s*. Princeton, NJ: Princeton University Press.

Gautier Morin, J. (2019). The Keynesian-Monetarist Competition over Public Credibility. *The Tocqueville Review*, 40(2), 281–294.

Gautier Morin, J., & Rossier, T. (2021). The Interaction of Elite Networks in the Pinochet Regime's Macroeconomic Policies. *Global Networks*, 21(2), 339–364.

Gerth, H., & Mills, C. W. (1953). *Character and Social Structure*. New York: Harcourt Brace Jovanovich.

Gill, R., & Scharff, C. (Eds.). (2011). *New Femininities: Postfeminism, Neoliberalism and Subjectivity*. London: Palgrave Macmillan.

Kapeller, J., Pühringer, S., & Grimm, C. (2021). Paradigms and Policies: The Current State of Economics in the German-Speaking Countries. *Review of International Political Economy* (online first). https://doi.org/10.1080/09692290.2021.1904269.

Hall, P. A. (Ed.). (1989). *The Political Power of Economic Ideas: Keynesianism across Nations*. Princeton, NJ: Princeton University Press.

Hirschman, D., & Popp Berman, E. (2014). Do Economists Make Policies? On the Political Effects of Economics. *Socio-Economic Review*, 12(4), 779–811.

Klüger, E. (2018). Mapping the Inflections in the Policies of the Brazilian National Economic and Social Development Bank during the 1990s and 2000s within Social Spaces and Networks. *Historical Social Research*, 43(3), 274–302.

Korom, P. (2020). How Do Academic Elites March through Departments? A Comparison of the Most Eminent Economists and Sociologists' Career Trajectories. *Minerva*, 58, 343–365.

Lebaron, F. (2000). *La croyance économique. Les économistes entre science et politique*. Paris: Editions du Seuil.

Lebaron, F. (2001). Economists and the Economic Order. The Field of Economists and the Field of Power in France. *European Societies*, 3(1), 91–110.

MacKenzie, D. A., Muniesa, F., & Siu, L. (Eds.). (2007). *Do Economists Make Markets? On the Performativity of Economics*. Princeton, NJ: Princeton University Press.

Maesse, J. (2015). Economic Experts: A Discursive Political Economy of Economics. *Journal of Multicultural Discourses*, 10(3), 279–305.

Maesse, J. (2018). Opening the Black Box of the Elitism Dispositif: Graduate Schools in Economics. In R. Bloch, A. Mitterle, C. Paradeise, & T. Peter (Eds.), *Universities and the Production of Elites: Discourses, Policies, and Strategies of Excellence and Stratification in Higher Education* (pp. 53–79). London: Palgrave Macmillan.

Maesse, J., Pahl, H., & Sparsam, J. (Eds.). (2017). *Die Innenwelt der Ökonomie: Wissen, Macht und Performativität in der Wirtschaftswissenschaft*. Berlin & Heidelberg: Springer.

Maesse, J., Pühringer, S., Rossier, T., & Benz, P. (2021a). The Role of Power in the Social Studies of Economics: An Introduction. In J. Maesse, S. Pühringer, T. Rossier, & P. Benz (Eds.), *Power and Influence of Economists: Contributions to the Social Studies of Economics* (pp. 1–15). London: Routledge (Taylor & Francis).

Maesse, J., Pühringer, S., Rossier, T., & Benz, P. (2021b). *Power and Influence of Economists: Contributions to the Social Studies of Economics*. London: Routledge (Taylor & Francis).

Mata, T., & Medema, S. (Eds.). (2013). *The Economist as Public Intellectual*. Durham: Duke University Press.

Miller, P. (2001). Governing by Numbers: Why Calculative Practices Matter. *Social Research*, 68(2), 379–396.

Mills, C. W. (2000 [1956]). *The Power Elite*. New York: Oxford University Press.

Mirowski, P. (1991). *More Heat Than Light: Economics as Social Physics, Physics as Nature's Economics*. Cambridge: Cambridge University Press.

Mirowski, P., & Plehwe, D. (Eds.) (2009). *The Road from Mont Pèlerin: The Making of the Neoliberal Thought Collective*. Cambridge, MA: Harvard University Press.

Montecinos, V., & Markoff, J. (2009). *Economists in the Americas.* Cheltenham: Edward Elgar.

Morgan, M. S. (1990). *The History of Econometric Ideas.* Cambridge: Cambridge University Press.

Önder, A. S., & Terviö, M. (2015). Is Economics a House Divided? Analysis of Citation Networks. *Economic Inquiry,* 53(3), 1491–1505.

Ötsch, W. O., Pühringer, S., & Hirte, K. (2017). *Netzwerke des Marktes: Ordoliberalismus als Politische Ökonomie.* Berlin & Heidelberg: Springer.

Pühringer, S. (2020). Think Tank Networks of German Neoliberalism. Power Structures in Economics and Economic Policies in Post-War Germany. In D. Plehwe, Q. Slobodian, & P. Mirowski (Eds.), *Nine Lives of Neoliberalism* (pp. 283–307). Brooklyn, NY: Verso.

Pühringer, S., & Griesser, M. (2020). From the 'Planning Euphoria' to the 'Bitter Economic Truth': The Transmission of Economic Ideas into German Labour Market Policies in the 1960s and 2000s. *Critical Discourse Studies,* 17(5), 476–493.

Rossier, T. (2020). Accumulation and Conversion of Capitals in Professorial Careers. The Importance of Scientific Reputation, Network Relations, and Internationality in Economics and Business Studies. *Higher Education,* 80, 1061–1080.

Rossier, T., & Buhlmann, F. (2018). The Internationalisation of Economics and Business Studies: Import of Excellence, Cosmopolitan Capital Or American Dominance? *Historical Social Research,* 43(3), 189–215.

Rossier, T., Buhlmann, F., & Mach, A. (2017). The Rise of Professors of Economics and Business Studies in Switzerland: Between Scientific Reputation and Political Power. *European Journal of Sociology,* 58(2), 295–326.

Salas-Porras, A., & Murray, G. (Eds.). (2017). *Think Tanks and Global Politics: Key Spaces in the Structure of Power.* London: Macmillan.

Savage, M., Warde, A., & Devine, F. (2005). Capitals, Assets, and Resources: Some Critical Issues. *British Journal of Sociology,* 56(1), 31–47.

Schmidt-Wellenburg, C. (2018). Struggling over Crisis. Discursive Positionings and Academic Positions in the Field of German-Speaking Economists. *Historical Social Research,* 43(3), 147–188.

Schmidt-Wellenburg, C., & Lebaron, F. (Eds.). (2018a). Economists, Politics, and Society. New Insights from Mapping Economic Practices Using Field-Analysis. *Historical Social Research, Special Issue,* 43(3), 7–38.

Schmidt-Wellenburg, C., & Lebaron, F. (2018b). There Is No Such Thing as "the Economy". Economic Phenomena Analysed from a Field-Theoretical Perspective. *Historical Social Research,* 43(3), 7–38.

Zuidhof, P. W. (2012). *Imagining Markets: The Discursive Politics of Neoliberalism.* Rotterdam: Erasmus University Rotterdam.

3

WHAT DO PEOPLE KNOW ABOUT ECONOMICS … AND WHAT SHOULD THEY KNOW?

Anna Killick

Introduction

> Experts agree: The typical voter knows next to nothing about politics, economics, or policy.
>
> *Bryan Caplan, economist (2013)*

> The political ignorance of the American voter is one of the best-documented features of contemporary politics.
>
> *Larry Bartels, political scientist (1996, p. 194)*

> For as long as we've been measuring, the mean, model, and median voters have been misinformed or ignorant about basic political information; they have known even less about more advanced social scientific knowledge.
>
> *Jason Brennan, political philosopher (2016, p. ix)*

One of the most dominant beliefs underpinning the political science and economics disciplines is that members of the public have a low level of political and economic knowledge, which has not risen during the decades since the 1960s that social scientists have been measuring it (Pew, 2007; European Commission, 2015; OECD, 2017; Haldane and McMahon, 2018; Galvao et al., 2019; YouGov et al., 2020).

This belief in the low level of public economic knowledge is not just an arcane academic issue; it has significant real-world effects. First, as anyone reflecting on judgements that have been made about their knowledge will agree, doing badly in a test is demoralising and can undermine confidence. Women, those on lower incomes and those with fewer years in education consistently achieve lower scores in knowledge tests than their counterparts (Walstad and Rebeck, 2002;

DOI: 10.4324/9781003283447-5

Lusardi and Mitchell, 2014; Vicente and Lopez, 2017; OECD, 2017; Haldane and McMahon, 2018). These groups may become aware that social scientists and other commentators believe that they lack knowledge, which may demotivate them further when it comes to economic or political engagement. Second, many social scientists believe that the low level of knowledge of the population as a whole damages economies in two ways – by the aggregative effects of poorly informed financial decisions on the economy and by the indirect effects of poorly informed choices about economic policies at the ballot box. The damage to economies is one factor that encourages some social scientists to advocate restricting democracy to the knowledgeable. In recent years, and particularly since what many social scientists have judged as the undesirable victories for Brexit and Donald Trump in 2016, backed disproportionately by people from two of the three 'low knowledge' demographic groups, there has been increased interest in restricting the franchise. Either this restriction in the franchise is to be achieved by stealth, not attempting to redress the correlation between low income and low turnout, or openly, such as advocating knowledge tests for voters (Caplan, 2013; Brennan, 2016; see also Somin, 2013).

Given the real-world effects, it is of vital importance that research conducted into public economic knowledge yields accurate results including recognising the limitations of the various methods used. In this chapter, my primary focus is on research methods because they are so central to the study of public economic knowledge. The methods researchers use will both reflect how they conceive of knowledge and have a profound effect on the kinds of results they get. I identify two main types of empirical research. First, the mainstream and still dominant approach that aims to measure 'levels' of knowledge, usually factual and using quantitative methods. Second, I turn to critics of the 'levels' approach, who lean towards investigating what people do know, rather than the facts they do not know, often using more bottom-up and qualitative methods and being cautious about making claims about 'how much' people know. But I also argue that it may be time to develop a new approach that synthesises some of the strengths of the two strands. Finally, and relatedly, I attempt to address the difficult question of whether and how we can research what is important for people to know about the economy.

'Levels' of Knowledge Approach

There are many similarities in the approach that political scientists and economists take to the study of economic knowledge because they both share an interest in how economic knowledge affects political behaviour. The 'first wave' of research into public economic knowledge across both disciplines has the following defining features:

- a belief that social scientists can judge what economic knowledge is useful for citizens to have,

- a belief that quantitative methods are the most effective way to measure knowledge because they allow for large samples and longitudinal study, and
- relatedly, a belief that 'factual' knowledge is useful for citizens to have, which has the added advantage that it can be measured using quantitative methods.

The most influential guide for political scientists has been Michael Delli Carpini and Scott Keeter's 1996 book, *What Americans Know and Why It Matters*, which refined existing methodological approaches from the Converse era and attempted to systematise research. However, they did not cover knowledge of economics in much depth, arguing that people who were knowledgeable about one domain such as civics-style politics questions, would tend to be knowledgeable about another, like foreign or economic affairs. Despite wanting to research economic knowledge in greater depth, economists have nevertheless mirrored the political scientists' methodological approach, for instance asking about 'measurable facts' and using a multiple-choice-style format.

One of the leading economists in this field is William Walstad, who launched a survey in 1992 on 'economic literacy' in the American National Election Study that became a regular study (Walstad and Larsen, 1992; Walstad and Rebeck, 2002, adapted by Evans in 2015). His objective was to assess economic knowledge 'about basic economic topics that arise in discussions of the national economy and economic events' (1992, p. 1226). He included factual questions about indicators, such as the size of the federal deficit, questions that tested definitions of terms, like 'GDP' or 'deficit' and broader ones about how inflation and growth are measured, how 'monetary policy' and 'fiscal policy' are set and what they mean. Walstad's verdict is 'unfortunately, most Americans know very little about economics' (1992, p. 1226).

Economists have often ranged further from the political scientists' preoccupation with the 'factual', by exploring what the public understands about how the economy works and the laws of economics. For example, in his 1997 survey, as well as asking the factual questions, Walstad asked, all using multiple choice, what economic policy would most likely be used to combat a recession during a period of low inflation, which of several factors listed would be likely to improve the wages of American workers, and what is 'the basic purpose of profits in our market economy'? On trade, he asked,

> Does setting quotas on foreign goods imported into the U.S. increase the number of jobs for Americans in the long-run?

He gave respondents two possible answers: 'yes' or 'no' (Walstad, 1997, p. 204). According to most neo-classically trained economists who understand the law of comparative advantage, 'no' is the correct answer, but many members of the public disagreed. Often, economists have jointly surveyed economists and members of the public to measure the extent of the gap between 'lay' and 'expert' beliefs (Caplan, 2001, 2002; Sapienza and Zingales, 2013). Economists are concerned about the size of the gap. Many have concluded that members of the public who have not been trained in what are often counter-intuitive economics laws exhibit not just lack of factual knowledge about the size of the federal budget and so on, but also systematic misperceptions or biases, such as being 'anti-trade' (Caplan, 2002, 2007; Haferkamp et al., 2009).

Critiques of the 'Levels' Approach

The strength of the first-wave studies is that the quantitative methods engender large socially representative samples and allow for a longitudinal study. However, since the 1990s, criticisms began to mount. The first charge centred on elitism (Graber, 2001; Lupia, 2006). How did social scientists decide which questions to include? Delli Carpini and Keeter's answer that 'the selection of specific items remains fairly subjective, guided by the goals of the research and influenced by factors not easily quantified' (1996, p. 299), did not inspire confidence that transparent criteria were being followed. Subjectivity can lead to what Lupia describes as 'a self-serving worldview', where researchers do not interrogate themselves about how their own socio-economic status may be affecting their judgement. Lupia (2006, p. 219) argues

> the elitist move is when such people assume that these questions have a similar value to citizens whose societal responsibilities can be very different from their own. When writers make this elitist move, they can switch from facilitating outcomes from which the voter or society will benefit to imposing on citizens a worldview whose relationship to such outcomes is speculative, at best.

Lupia concluded that people only needed 'sufficient' knowledge to make 'competent' decisions, which might include following cues or heuristics.

One by-product of the elitism is that researchers' subjectivity and narrowness of worldview can lead them to design tests that skew the results of certain demographic groups, leading to exaggerated judgements about how little they know. While scholars have put some effort into rectifying a perceived gender bias in knowledge tests (Dolan, 2011; Fraile and Gomez, 2015; Pérez, 2015), the 'income bias' is arguably greater and relatively neglected. Research into 'financial' knowledge serves as an example. Most social scientists accept the definition of financial knowledge as the 'ability to use knowledge and skills to manage financial resources effectively for a lifetime of financial well-being'.[1] However, the British Elections Study (BES) (Fieldhouse, 2018) chooses to assess financial knowledge on the basis of three questions about savings and investments, which many people on low incomes have less personal experience of than those on higher incomes. This researchers' choice to focus on savings and investment, rather than more universal financial skills like budgeting, prejudices low-income respondents' chance to show their financial knowledge. Researchers have sometimes used these skewed knowledge test results to explain why people have particular attitudes, for example, to immigration (Panos and Wright, 2015).

Second, in the case of many economists' research to test knowledge of economic laws like comparative advantage, the questions reflect a 'narrow definition' of economic understanding based on neoclassical economic theory (Boyer and Petersen, 2018). They may gloss over divisions between economists, which became more heightened following the 2008 financial crisis (Evans, 2015). In addition, unlike some concepts from natural sciences, economic terms have 'common meanings' and are used extensively by average citizens in their everyday lives (Darriet and Bourgeois-Gironde, 2015). When citizens use words such as 'consumption' or 'unemployment', they may acquire a different meaning, compared with how economists understand it. Tests based on neoclassical economists' worldviews prevent us from finding out more about this kind of knowledge.

What People Know Rather Than How Much

Some researchers have argued that people's understanding of economics should also be explored through a 'bottom-up approach' to explore what they know, gathering more discursive evidence about why they think the way they do. This approach has three main features:

- The researcher approaches questioning with an open mind about what constitutes 'knowledge'.
- The questions are open-ended; allowing respondents to talk about what they know, think they know and also think they might not know or understand, and why.
- The researcher uses interpretivist approaches to analyse and identifies the patterns and themes that emerge in the field rather than testing pre-existing theories (Killick 2020).

I give three examples of this approach. First, the American scholar of public economic understanding Katharine Cramer identified what she called a 'politics of resentment' in rural Wisconsin (2016). Cramer started as a quantitative researcher, arriving at interviews with a sheaf of scripted questions with multiple-choice answers (Cramer Walsh, 2009). However, often, as she reached the end of the interview and turned the recording device off, her interviewees would start to chat, telling her which questions they had found difficult or what they really thought about aspects that the questions had not touched on. She valued how in the chats, 'neither I nor the authors of the survey were setting the agenda or framing the range of possible responses'. Instead, her interviewees

> explained themselves to me in their own words. They strung their thoughts together in packages and structures that had meaning to them, if not necessarily to researchers designing a nationwide survey.

(p. 170)

Because she learned so much from the chat, she started to supplement her quantitative methods with more inductive studies into what people know, expressed in their own words and terms. Cramer chose the ethnographic approach of 'gate-crashing' existing social groups by having coffee and trying to introduce questions on key topics but then interjecting as little as possible (2016). Cramer used interpretivist methods to analyse the transcripts and concluded that her respondents did not 'lack' economic knowledge, but allowed their cultural beliefs about city-dwellers to get in the way of a more rational analysis of how economic policies affected them.

I used a similar approach to Cramer in my UK-based study of how members of the public from a range of backgrounds following the 2016 referendum viewed the phenomenon of 'the economy', although unlike Cramer I used interviews instead of group talk (Killick 2020). I phrased questions about aspects of the economy using the neutral 'what do you think you know about employment, inflation, trade and so on?'. I also concluded that people see the economy through the lens of their own experience (Cramer 2016; Cramer and Toff, 2017). There is a gulf between how high- and low-income people see the economy, which is based less on factual knowledge than how they and their personalised and localised positions stand in relation to the official version.

Other qualitative scholars have used more prescribed methods to analyse, such as coding manuals that can be replicated. William Gamson (1992), for example, in his seminal study of political consciousness gathers social groups from low-income backgrounds, encouraging them to discuss four topics in-depth, that includes the 'economic' topic of factory closures. Like most qualitative researchers in this area, Gamson does not conclude with a 'level' of knowledge, other than to argue that his respondents countered the fact test evidence of low knowledge; 'people are not so dumb' (1992, p. 4).

One weakness of qualitative study is obviously the small-scale nature of it, combined with the lack of replicability over time and between locations. In addition, some quantitative researchers might object that interpretivist methods give too much freedom of manoeuvre to the qualitative researcher in how they analyse the dominant themes that 'emerge' from the interviews or group discussions. Therefore, quantitative 'levels of' economic knowledge researchers should continue to conduct surveys, but they could improve them in two ways. First, they could attempt to contextualise what people know. I focus on practical suggestions. I urge quantitative researchers to be more rigorous in questioning what may be their own narrow worldviews by choosing questions that tap into a broader range of personal experiences, minimum wage levels as well as investments. Cramer (2009) suggests they use open-ended questions more within the survey instrument. She also suggests that where they conduct interviews face to face, they could supplement the data with rich observations of the place in which respondents live, and could strive for longer interview sessions that encourage and allow time to record respondents' own interpretations. Second, could they be less definitive in the way they report their findings? They are not establishing levels of knowledge but responses to researcher-chosen items of factual knowledge.

Mixed method studies that allow researchers to compare and probe survey findings in interviews or focus groups may also be illuminating (Williamson and Wearing, 1996; Graber, 2003). One exemplar is the UK's ESCOE report in collaboration with the Office for National Statistics entitled 'Public understanding of economics and economic statistics' (Runge and Hudson, 2020). They conducted 12 focus groups, asking participants similar questions to those they asked in a nationally representative survey of 1665 people. The questions covered topics like employment, interest rates, trade, deficit, debt, inflation and GDP. The authors argue that there are widespread 'misperceptions' but less on some topics (interest rates) than others (GDP). While the survey showed the usual low level of knowledge, the focus groups added additional insights, such as that

> Participants understood economic issues through the lens of their familiar 'personal economy' rather than the abstract 'national economy'. This meant that while focus group participants often demonstrated detailed knowledge about, and interest in, the personal impacts of economic indicators, they often struggled to relate this to the broader economy.
>
> *(p. 4)*

One of the virtues of ESCOE's, admittedly detailed and cost-intensive study, is that rather than just 'measuring' knowledge it also generates insights for policymakers, communicators and statisticians about how they could communicate more effectively, thus potentially increasing public understanding.

What Is It Important to Know?

Researching with the aim of establishing what it is *important* for citizens to know about the economy is less justifiable than descriptive research that maps what they do and do not know because it inevitably involves value judgement. Bartels (2005) asks whether low-income voters supporting President Bush's tax cuts may have been confused about their own interests. Lupia (2006) suggests that people need 'sufficient' knowledge to be competent voters. But neither suggests the benchmark economic knowledge which would be desirable for all citizens to have. Even the economists most disturbed by the gap between their own knowledge and that of the public have been reluctant to stipulate what content of knowledge a citizen needs. The design of their tests suggests the kind of thing they have in mind, and they often advocate for more effective teaching of economic literacy in schools (Walstad and Larsen, 1992; Walstad and Rebuck, 2002). But at the adult level, even those such as Caplan who advocate 'knowledge tests' for voters opt for 'civics-style' questions, rather than economics ones (2013).

We could conduct research that asks people what they think is important to know. Runge and Hudson (2020) ask this question in focus groups and establish that, for instance, interest rates seem important to those with mortgages. Two members of a focus group have this exchange about what they think is important:

> From my point of view... two big indicators for, what you might call the average working people, I think, are wage growth and inflation... Those two, in particular, sort of influence a lot of our financial decisions, the day to day living. If wage growth is fairly stagnant, and yet inflation's going up...
>
> They're more prominent in our lives, aren't they?
>
> *(2020, pp. 51–52)*

However, this kind of bottom-up research could not arrive at a settled evidence-based consensus about what citizens believe is important they should know about the economy. The task of establishing any benchmarks for what is important inevitably involves some researcher input, with the dangers of introducing an element of subjectivity that implies.

Conclusion

In conclusion, methodologically, in economic knowledge research, there is an over-reliance on closed multiple-choice-style survey questions, which may not give the full picture of what people do and do not know and why. Excessive reliance on such methods also misses opportunities for policy-makers and communicators to learn the kinds of lessons that qualitative methods can teach them about how they might communicate the economic knowledge they possess more effectively. Some quantitative researchers may argue that qualitative researchers' reluctance to arrive at definitive judgements about 'levels' of knowledge is a failing and smacks of relativism, denying the value of possessing accurate factual knowledge and understanding of expert theories. However, they should consider being more precise and qualified about the claims they make; they are only measuring knowledge of selected facts and cannot extrapolate from that to make the broader claim about people, or groups of people, that they are economically 'uninformed' or 'lack knowledge'.

Digging Deeper

Discussion Questions

1. How do we know what people know about economics?
2. Who should be able to say what is important for people to know about economics?

Suggested Further Reading

Irwin, A., & Michael, M. (2003). 'The public understanding of science and technology: from cognition to context.' In *Science, Social Theory & Public Knowledge* (pp. 19–40). Maidenhead, U.K. and Philadelphia, PA: Open University Press and McGraw-Hill Education.

Suldovsky, B. (2016). 'In science communication, why does the idea of the public deficit always return? Exploring key influences.' *Public Understanding of Science*, 25(4), 415–426.

Note

1 Used by the USA President's Advisory Council on Financial Capability (Panos and Wright 2015).

References

Bartels, L. (1996). 'Uninformed votes: information effects in presidential elections.' *American Political Science Review*, 40, 194–230.

Bartels, L. (2005). 'Homer gets a tax cut: inequality and public policy in the American mind'. *Perspectives on Politics*, 3(1), 15–31. Published by: American Political Science Association Stable. URL: https://www.jstor.org/stable/3688108.

Boyer, P., & Petersen, M. B. (2018). 'Folk-economic beliefs: an evolutionary cognitive model.' *Behavioral and Brain Sciences*, 41, e158. doi: 10.1017/S0140525X17001960.

Brennan, J. (2016). *Against Democracy*. Princeton, NJ: Princeton University Press.

Caplan, B. (2001). 'What makes people think like economists? Evidence on economic cognition from the "Survey of Americans and Economists on the Economy".' *Journal of Law and Economics*, 44(2), 395–426.

Caplan, B. (2002). 'Systematically biased beliefs about economics: robust evidence of judgemental anomalies from the survey of Americans and economists on the economy.' *The Economic Journal*, 112(April), 433–458.

Caplan, B. (2007). *The Myth of the Rational Voter: Why Democracies Choose Bad Policies*. Princeton, NJ: Princeton University Press.

Caplan, B. (2013). 'A cheap, inoffensive way to make democracy work better'. Library of Economics and Liberty Website, econlog.econlib.org/archives/2013/10/a_ cheap_ inoffen.html.

Cramer, K. (2016). *The Politics of Resentment: Rural Consciousness in Wisconsin and the Rise of Scott Walker*. Chicago, IL: University of Chicago Press.

Cramer, K., & Toff, B. (2017). 'The fact of experience: rethinking political knowledge and civic competence.' *Perspectives on Politics*, 15(3), 754–770.

Cramer Walsh, K. (2009). 'Scholars as citizens: studying public opinion through ethnography.' In E. Schatz (Ed.), *Political Ethnography: What Immersion Contributes to the Study of Power* (pp. 165–182), Chicago: University of Chicago Press.

Darriet, E., & Bourgeois-Gironde, S. (2015). 'Why lay social representations of the economy should count in economics.' *Mind and Society*, 14(2), 245–258.

Delli Carpini, M., & Keeter, S. (1996). *What Americans Know about Politics and Why It Matters*. New Haven, CT: Yale University Press.

Dolan, K. (2011). 'Do women and men know different things? Measuring gender differences in political knowledge.' *The Journal of Politics*, 73(1), 97–107.

Evans, B. (2015). 'Did economic literacy influence macroeconomic policy preferences of the general public during the financial crisis?' *The American Economist*, 60(2), 132–141.

Fieldhouse, E., Green, J., Evans, G., Schmitt, H., van der Eijk, C., Mellon, J., & Prosser, C. (2018). 'British election study internet panel waves 1–14.' Available at: http://www.britishelectionstudy.com/data-objects/panel-stdy-data/.

Fraile, M., & Gomez, R. (2015). 'Why does Alejandro know more about politics than Catalina? Explaining the Latin American gender gap in political knowledge.' *British Journal of Political Science*, 47(1), 1–22.

Galvao, A., Mitchell, J., & Runge, J. (2019). 'Communicating data uncertainty: experimental evidence for U.K. GDP.' Economic Statistics Centre of Excellence (ESCoE) Discussion Papers ESCoE DP-2019-20. https://ideas.repec.org/p/nsr/escoed/escoe-dp-2019-20.html.

Gamson, W. (1992). *Talking Politics*. Cambridge: Cambridge University Press.

Graber, D. (2001). *Processing Politics: Learning from Television in the Internet Age*. Chicago, IL: University of Chicago Press.

Graber, D. (2003). 'The media and democracy beyond myths and stereotypes.' *Annual Review Political Science*, 6, 139–160. doi: 10.1146/annurev.polisci.6.121901.085707.

Haferkamp, A., Fetchenhauer, D., Belschak, F., & Enste, D. (2009). 'Efficiency versus fairness: the evaluation of labor market policies by economists and laypeople.' *Journal of Economic Psychology*, 30(4), 527–539.

Haldane, A., & McMahon, M. (2018). 'Central Bank communications and the general public.' *AEA Papers and Proceedings*, 108, 578–583.

Killick, A. (2020). *Rigged: Understandings of 'the Economy' in Brexit Britain*. Manchester: Manchester University Press.

Lupia, A. (2006). 'How elitism undermines the study of voter competence.' *Critical Review*, 18(1–3), 217–232. doi: 10.1080/08913810608443658.

Lusardi, A., & Mitchell, O. (2014). 'The economic importance of financial literacy: theory and evidence.' *Journal of Economic Literature*, 52(1), 5–44.

OECD (2017). 'G20/OECD INFE report on adult financial literacy in G20 countries.' https://www.oecd.org/finance/g20-oecd-infe-report-adult-financial-literacy-in-g20-countries.htm.

Panos, G., & Wright, R. (2015). 'Financial literacy and attitudes towards immigration British election study 23/03/2015.' https://www.britishelectionstudy.com/bes-impact/financial-literacy-and-attitudes-towards-immigration/#.YXaQv_nMJRM.

Pérez, E. O. (2015). 'Mind the gap: why large group deficits in political knowledge emerge—and what to do about them.' *Political Behavior*, 37(4), 933–954.

Pew Research centre (2007). 'Public knowledge of current affairs little changed by news information revolutions: what Americans know 1989-2007 report April 15 2007.' https://www.pewresearch.org/politics/2007/04/15/public-knowledge-of-current-affairs-little-changed-by-news-and-information-revolutions/.

Runge, J., & Hudson, N. (2020). Public Understanding of Economics and Economic Statistics ESCoE Occasional Paper 03.

Sapienza, P., & Zingales, L. (2013). 'Economic experts versus average Americans.' *The American Economic Review*, 103(3), 636–642. doi: 10.1257/aer.103.3.636.

Somin, I. (2013). *Democracy and Political Ignorance*. Stanford, CA: Stanford University Press.

Vicente, M., & Lopez, A. (2017). 'Figuring figures: exploring Europeans' knowledge of official economic statistics.' *Journal of Official Statistics*, 33(4), 1051–1085.

Walstad, W. B. (1997). 'The effect of economic knowledge on public opinion of economic issues.' *Journal of Economic Education*, 28(3), 195–205. Retrieved from https://www.proquest.com/scholarly-journals/effect-economic-knowledge-on-public-opinion/docview/62539164/se-2?accountid=14511.

Walstad, W., & Larsen, M. (1992). *A National Survey of American Economic Literacy*. Lincoln, NE: The Gallup Organization.

Walstad, W. B., & Rebeck, K. (2002). 'Assessing the economic knowledge and economic opinions of adults.' *Quarterly Review of Economics and Finance*, 42, 921–935.

Williamson, M., & Wearing, A. (1996). 'Lay people's cognitive models of the economy.' *Economic Psychology*, 17(1), 3–38.

YouGov and National Institute for Economic and Social Research (February 2020), Economic Knowledge Survey, https://docs.cdn.yougov.com/avbj6q6w62/NIESR_EconomicsKnowledge_w.pdf.

SECTION TWO
How to Make Economics Public?

Let us start this section with some dates.

*   1752 – the year the (arguably) first science museum was opened – the Museo Nacional de Ciencias Naturales in Madrid.
*   1959 – the year St. Louis got its own interactive science museum, the Museum of Science and Natural History.
*   2006 – the year the world's first economics museum was opened, the Museo Interactivo de Economía in México City.
*   2014 – the year the St. Louis Federal Reserve opened its own economics museum.

We mention these dates to highlight two things vital to this section of the book. One, economics has been late to the party when it comes to practical efforts to becoming more accessible and explorable by the public. And two, new and exciting things are happening worldwide. The day-to-day hard work of the people behind these initiatives is even more impressive when we notice the relative lack of others doing similar around them and the lack of institutional support they receive as compared, say, with the public understanding of science movement. Count the economics museums, documentaries and festivals, and then compare that number with that of science museums, documentaries and festivals, and you'll see the point. The authors in this section, and those driving these and other endeavours to make economics more public, are passionate about the need to link publics with economics. Key to all their work is making connections – through media, through interactive museum exhibits, through communicative networks and through broadening assumptions about what economics is and how it is taught.

DOI: 10.4324/9781003283447-6

In this section, we will see four forms which this effort has taken.

In the first chapter of this section, Chapter 4, public-facing economist Romesh Vaitilingam discusses, from the inside, how several organisations, including the Royal Economic Society media initiative, VoxEU and the Economics Observatory, have used their media- and online-savvy to make links between economic research and a variety of publics, from policy makers to school children.

Chapter 5, by Thomas Shepherd and Eva Johnston, is about how museum exhibits, in particular, at the St. Louis Economy Museum, can link audiences to concepts. This is especially tricky when the concepts are seemingly abstract, and museum staff need to find ways to make them feel concrete to visitors. Inside the Economy Museum, the key aim is that people leave having reflected upon the ways they play a daily role in the economy and the ways in which economics is a ubiquitous part of their daily life, an understanding that they come to by hands-on interactions with exhibits.

In Chapter 6, the Rethinking Economics team presents its vision for economics. They are a global network of critical economists working to build and support a wider range of conversations among and between citizens, students, policy makers and academics. These links seek inclusivity to broaden the stories we tell about economics and serve as an example of how economics can itself work.

Lastly, in Chapter 7, Christopher Colvin shows readers a compulsory first-year university course that he designed and teaches. In it he helps students learn to communicate about economics, in part by exploring the idea that economics has a multiple nature. He helps them see ways in which economics is not only science, but also literature, politics, history and philosophy. This is an active course in communication, aiming to help economists of the future think about economics – and talk about it too.

4

PUBLIC-FACING ECONOMISTS

Romesh Vaitilingam

Getting research written up in the media or being used to provide expert comments on news stories is a good leading indicator of an economist's impact on the wider world. A comment once made to me by Julian Le Grand, London School of Economics (LSE) professor and former prime ministerial adviser, is representative of the typical view among UK parliamentarians and senior civil servants:

> In getting attention in Westminster/Whitehall and having a major policy impact, getting into the press is absolutely central. Press briefings summarising relevant pieces are circulated once a day around No. 10, etc. An article on new research by, for example, Nick Timmins at the *Financial Times* is worth its weight in gold.
>
> *(Personal Correspondence, 2006)*

Yet academic economists in the UK and elsewhere in Europe have often been accused of hiding out in their ivory towers and not engaging with the popular media with the same enthusiasm as their American counterparts – people like economics Nobel laureate–cum–*New York Times* columnist Paul Krugman or Steven 'Freakonomics' Levitt. There is some truth in this view, and it partly reflects a lack of resources: getting involved with the media requires organisational commitment and support, which are rarely forthcoming in European universities. It also reflects weak incentives: despite the efforts of research funding agencies to encourage scholars to communicate their findings to wide audiences, the real rewards come from communicating with one's peers and that means technical articles in top journals.

Happily though, some research institutions have shown that is possible to combine rigorous economic scholarship with being 'in the news' – as well as having significant influence on policy and practice. In the UK, for example,

DOI: 10.4324/9781003283447-7

staff and associates of the Institute for Fiscal Studies (IFS) and the Centre for Economic Performance (CEP) at LSE are often found on press comment pages, providing expert insight into broadcast news stories or actively promoting their expertise in blogs and on social media. In contrast with the many economists who seem reluctant to package their findings in a way that will attract an audience beyond academia, IFS and CEP have always sought to buck this trend: one of their central aims is for top-quality economic research to have an impact on society through the long-term percolation of new ideas into policy, practice and public understanding.

Over the past two decades, there has also been a series of cross-institutional and cross-national initiatives in Europe to encourage economists to become more public facing and to support them in that endeavour. The very first was set up in Italy by Tito Boeri in 2002 in response to a national media landscape then dominated by Silvio Berlusconi: La Voce was the original economics policy portal and the inspiration for VoxEU, set up by the Centre for Economic Policy Research (CEPR, a global network of research economists) in the summer of 2007 to provide 'research-based policy analysis and commentary from leading economists' (Baldwin, 2020). Even before then in the mid-1990s, the Royal Economic Society (RES, the professional association of UK economists) launched a 'media initiative', in part as a way to attract more young people to study economics and provide future generations of economic researchers and policy advisers.

More recently, in response to demand from policy-makers and the public to answers to pressing questions around the pandemic, a group of UK economists launched a project to bridge the gap between academic research, government policy and the general public. As the Economic Observatory website explains,

> Our goal is to provide balanced and reliable answers to the economic questions that Covid-19 and its aftermath will bring. We make it our mission to make these answers as accessible and engaging as possible. The team is drawn from across the nations and regions of the UK, with a hub in Bristol. By publishing daily articles, videos and charts, we believe the Observatory can help the public and policy-makers better understand the pandemic and the numerous challenges that will follow.
>
> *(Economics Observatory, 2022)*

I was involved in the launches of the RES initiative, the VoxEU policy portal and the Economics Observatory, and the following outlines the thinking behind their establishment, what they have achieved to date and some lessons for economists who would like to be more public facing.

The Royal Economic Society Media Initiative

The RES media initiative launched in early 1996 with initial financial support from the Economic and Social Research Council (ESRC), the UK's public agency funding research in the social sciences. Its overall aim was to promote the public profile of the Society and the economics profession more broadly via the press, broadcast and online media – to communicate research findings and expertise to people who can make use of them, to enhance the public understanding of economics and to attract young people to study the discipline to provide the next generation of economists in the UK. It was the brainchild of then RES secretary-general Richard Portes (also the founder of CEPR in the early 1980s), together with the late Tony Atkinson and David Hendry, both RES presidents during the 1990s.

At the heart of the RES media strategy was a steady stream of press releases to a database of journalists. These 'media briefings' summarised in a punchy and accessible form the findings of research projects, either those published in books, working papers, scholarly journals (like the Society's own *Economic Journal*) or special reports prepared for a wider audience or which were presented at academic conferences or public events. They were eventually circulated to a database of nearly 800 journalists and bloggers in the UK, continental Europe and North America, initially by mail and later, as new communications technologies emerged, by email and social media. Tailored versions of the briefings were also sent to targeted groups of journalists – and circulated to all government economists and school teachers of economics and related subjects.

As the RES media consultant from the launch of the initiative until 2019, I also had a 'reactive' role, which partly involved advising individual academics and research institutions how and to whom in the media they might seek to promote their research. It also involved providing journalists with researchers to advise them on particular news stories or features. After the global financial crisis of 2007–2009, this stream of enquiries (which used to be at least twice each week) increased substantially – not just from core economic journalists but also from a much wider global community of journalists. From 2013, I also promoted RES output via social media, notably Twitter.

The RES initiative enjoyed great success: the media response to the economics profession's efforts to increase coverage of its output was overwhelmingly positive, generating much coverage and indicating that there is a large appetite for economic research delivered in a user-friendly way. At the same time, academic economists welcomed assistance in their dissemination efforts, responding well to the challenge of presenting their work in a form accessible to a wider, non-specialist audience.

Early on in the life of the RES media initiative, I wrote an article summarising the characteristics of economists' work that attracts the most media attention. This analysis – which Roger Middleton quoted in his 1998 book *Charlatans or Saviours? Economists and the British Economy from Marshall to Meade* – is worth reiterating here:

- The research covers subjects that are high or that frequently recur on the agenda of public conversation. These days, they might include work–life balance, GM foods, school quality and house prices, happiness and immigration.

- The research comes up with distinct and easily quantifiable results.
- The research has clear implications for government economic and social policy.
- The research provides novel perspectives on industries of general public interest, typically those whose products people really enjoy buying, such as restaurants, wine, gambling, films and music.
- The research offers an overarching perspective on great themes of modern concern like the impact of globalisation and new technology. (Middleton, 1998)

VoxEU and the Centre for Economic Policy Research

Founded 15 years ago by CEPR, the VoxEU site features daily columns by established and emerging members of the profession, which are accessed by a wide range of readers. The main target audiences in academia, think tanks, finance ministries and other government departments, central banks, international organisations and the media usually have at least a little economics training. But the idea is to avoid the equations and write in a succinct and readable way, with the key findings and policy implications upfront.

VoxEU was inspired by the success of the Italian language site, La Voce, founded by Tito Boeri. La Voce means 'the voice' in Italian, and this is what inspired the Vox name (Vox.org was taken at the time by a Facebook wannabe, so VoxEU.org became the chosen website address). La Voce is a collection of online opinion pieces, which are short and written for the average newspaper reader. Given the large number of English language blogs, Richard Baldwin (founding editor-in-chief and still the driving force behind the initiative) felt that VoxEU should aim more upmarket – that it should become more like a Brookings Papers for the twenty-first century, thus acting as a bridge between technical, academic economics and the wider universe of people interested in economics.

The first few months of VoxEU were a success of sorts. This was almost guaranteed given the founding contributors: Philippe Aghion, the late Alberto Alesina, Richard Baldwin, Erik Berglöf, Giuseppe Bertola, Tim Besley, Olivier Blanchard, Tito Boeri, Willem Buiter, Michael Burda, Stephen Cecchetti, Daniel Cohen, Mathias Dewatripont, Juan Dolado, Esther Duflo, Barry Eichengreen, Jeffrey Frankel, Francesco Giavazzi, Rachel Griffith, Philip Lane, Philippe Martin, Richard Portes, Anne Sibert, Guido Tabellini, Shang-Jin Wei and Charles Wyplosz.

But as Richard Baldwin once put it, 'then we got lucky, as the world got unlucky' (Baldwin, 2017). The global financial crisis is what really gave VoxEU a large, loud voice in the world of economic research and policy. While the site was well read before the US subprime crisis, August 2007 was when our readership really took off. In the autumn of 2007, things seemed incomprehensible to most economists, journalists and policy-makers; writers like Stephen Cecchetti rode to the rescue by explaining exactly what was happening. His column on it, 'Federal Reserve policy actions in August 2007: frequently asked questions (updated)' set a standard for serious economics applied to the crisis, when most economic journalists and opinion column writers were talking about 'liquidity problems' (Cecchetti, 2007).

When Lehman Brothers went down in September 2008 and threatened to take the US and global economies with it, VoxEU again shone. The world, it seemed, had changed in ways that only a few experts understood, and even the experts did not see all the pieces. VoxEU became a vehicle for sharing this knowledge quickly and effectively – without having to write long reports or trying to dumb down complex ideas, facts and theories into 800-word newspaper opinion pieces. In late 2008, the crisis turned from a North Atlantic banking crisis into the global crisis via a massive trade shock. VoxEU's readership reached beyond the North Atlantic along with the crisis. In 2010, the eurozone crisis provided another boost, as did the shock outcome of the Brexit referendum and, most recently, the economic crisis sparked by the pandemic and the economic ramifications of Russia's invasion of Ukraine. VoxEU, in short, does well when economies do poorly.

VoxEU matches interesting writers and interested readers. This is beneficial to both. The world's best economists are driven by a desire to apply their brains, hard work and specialised knowledge in the interests of better informing the policy choices that affect people's everyday lives. The fact that VoxEU readers include a vast range of government officials, private sector economists, elite business and media professionals, and academics is a strong draw for the world's best, policy-relevant economists. That pins down the writer side. The reader side comes with the high-quality columns that VoxEU authors write every day.

The Economics Observatory

The seed of an idea that grew into the Economics Observatory was first planted and nurtured in a series of conversations in March 2020. In the wake of the pandemic, lockdown and what already looked likely to be the deepest recession in living memory, there was a growing sense that the UK's economic research community should come together to answer questions from policy-makers and the public about the economics of the coronavirus crisis and recovery.

With funding from ESRC and hosting for the pilot stage by IFS, it was possible to mobilise the expertise of economists from a wide range of universities and research institutions. At launch just a couple of months later, on 1 June 2020, 40 Q&A articles were published on the website, a number that has since grown to well over 550 by early 2022.

Many of the topics that were addressed initially were focused on the immediate crisis: what damage would lockdown and recession cause to people's physical and mental health? How would children and parents cope with school closures? Which firms and industries were being hit hardest? How did the government's job furlough scheme work? What was being done to protect the most vulnerable? And how might we end up paying for these big public policy interventions?

But the team of lead editors (Tim Besley, Jagjit Chadha, Diane Coyle, Huw Dixon, Rachel Griffith, Michael McMahon, Carol Propper, Graeme Roy, Sarah Smith and John Turner) also wanted to explore some long-term challenges raised by the pandemic, the recession and their aftermath: what will happen to big cities if there is a more permanent move to working from home? How can we make up for the learning losses suffered by a generation of children? And which policies might be most effective in tackling the high, and highly unequal, impact of the crisis on businesses, jobs, incomes and mental health.

Many people and organisations have contributed to Observatory's growth, not least ESRC and the University of Bristol, which is now hosting the hub. But recognition is particularly due to Rachel Griffith (IFS, Manchester and a recent past president of the RES), whose scholarship, dynamism and commitment to communicating economics made such a key contribution to the project's early development. Rachel is also a pioneer in teaching a course on communicating economics for undergraduate students.

The Economics Observatory aims to bring economics to the public in an accessible way. Similarly, the annual Festival of Economics in Bristol is a longstanding effort to engage with the public on economic issues central to their lives. The festival is co-programmed by Diane Coyle at Cambridge, who founded the event in 2012, and Observatory director Richard Davies at Bristol, the UK's first professor of the public understanding of economics.

Lessons

For economists wanting to write about their research for readers beyond their narrow specialism, VoxEU is a good starting point. Similar 'multi-authored blogs' open to new contributors include Ideas for India, the Economic Research Forum (covering the Middle East and North Africa) and The Long Run (established by the Economic History Society) – as well as several sites in languages other than English, including Nada es Gratis in Spain and Italy's La Voce.

Similarly, LSE has a suite of blogs – which cover economics, business and politics in a number of regions of the world – written at the level of *The Economist* or *Financial Times*, and which are generating a broad global readership. The editors are very open to ideas from researchers looking to try their hand at writing for non-specialist readers.

More advice on communicating economics through blogs, Twitter and so on is on the Communicating Economics website that I launched in 2017 together with Rachel Griffith and Bob Denham of Econ Films. The site includes many examples of the use of film and video as tools for communicating economics, as well as advice on making videos and how to perform well in front of a camera whether you're being interviewed by colleagues or a big broadcast organisation like the BBC. One notable piece explains the five steps involved in making an effective economics research video of under three minutes; another provides an example of how to explain your research in just 15 seconds.

Of course, all the principles of effective research communication go back well before the internet became ubiquitous. Whatever the communication channel, the best place to start is to write a short summary of the key findings of your research in a way that's accessible and appealing to someone who isn't trained in economics – something that you'd be happy to give to your spouse, your child or a non-economist friend. The notes I've long used on how to write a 'media briefing' summarising your working paper or conference presentation are on the site (Vaitilingam, 2020).

Communications Training for Economic Researchers

Some members of the Communicating Economics team and the Economics Observatory hub provide training for economists focused on opportunities to communicate their research findings and economic expertise to audiences beyond academia – to have more 'impact' on policy-makers, private sector decision-makers and the general public.

It is aimed at early and mid-career professional economists looking to develop their communication skills: translating detailed research and policy analysis into accessible messages for non-specialist audiences; writing clearly and presenting well in public speaking; and making effective use of broadcast media and social media. Courses and workshops, typically a half-day or full day, cover the following:

- Effective research dissemination: why it matters; the role of the media; engaging with the public and media agendas; making an impact outside academia; media success stories; developing a research programme's media and communications strategy.
- Thinking strategically about how to package your research findings and research-based policy analysis and commentary, when to release it, which audiences to target (policy-makers, private sector, the media, the general public) and how to respond to 'real-world' opportunities to intervene in public debates – for example, elections, referendums, European/international summits, economic data releases.
- Stories and press releases: key elements of news; the importance of narratives; using rhetoric and metaphor; positioning research for the media; placing stories; reacting to news, communicating with the press.
- Writing accessible versions of research papers and evidence surveys for different audiences: including VoxEU and other multi-authored blogs (for example, LSE's suite of blogs; the Conversation).
- Effective presentation to non-specialist audiences – how to summarise your findings and their significance in 5- to 10-minute presentations.
- Organising events to present research findings and analysis: public meetings; policy seminars with civil servants, politicians, etc.; working dinners with journalists – also taking advantage of publicity opportunities at academic

conferences, such as American Economic Association, the European Economic Association and the RES, and 'festival of economics'-type events like Bristol's.

- Establishing an effective Twitter presence: how to condense the message of your research in a way that attracts attention and stimulates productive discussions.
- Developing ideas for short films – for example, those posted on Vox Videos; how to do interviews well; different types of media interviews (TV/radio; live/pre-recorded; studio/down the line); conveying what you want to say rather than responding to someone else's agenda.

Final Word

Economic research institutions like IFS and CEP – as well as the cross-institutional initiatives by the RES, VoxEU and the Economics Observatory – show that it is possible not only to follow the rigorous intellectual pursuit of economics but also to illuminate the wider worlds of policy-making, private practice and public debate.

Nevertheless, there remains much to be done: there are powerful forces in society whose interests are challenged by scientific experts and which, therefore, seek to discredit them in the eyes of the public (the Leave campaign in the UK's Brexit referendum and 'anti-vaxxers' in the pandemic are two recent examples). What's more, surveys of representative samples of the public by ING and the Economics Network show the limitations of what has been achieved in improving the public understanding of economics (ING-Economics Network, 2019).

In addition to the efforts described above, a number of other overlapping initiatives are seeking to address particular audiences:

- Discover Economics is an RES campaign that aims to broaden the appeal of economics to potential university students, change perceptions of economics and economists and attract more young women and people from minority and state school backgrounds into the field. It is led by Sarah Smith at Bristol and Arun Advani at Warwick.
- CORE (Curriculum Open-access Resources in Economics) is an initiative launched after the global financial crisis reform in response to student pressures for a new introductory economics curriculum and the sense of a need for 'teaching economics as if the last three decades had happened' (Carlin, 2014). Led by Wendy Carlin at University College London and Samuel Bowles at the Santa Fe Institute, it seeks to change economics education globally to focus on the most important problems faced by our societies including climate change, injustice, innovation and the future of work; to put the student at the centre of pedagogy using learning materials and experiences attuned both to the social problems that students care about and to how students acquire facility and confidence in using and communicating economics; to make knowledge freely available on a global scale by

providing high-quality open access educational resources and to help change who studies economics to include more women and other underrepresented groups by changing content, pedagogy and access to knowledge.

- The Initiative on Global Markets (IGM) Forum at Chicago Booth has for just over a decade been regularly polling some of the world's top economic experts in the United States and Europe for their views on topical issues of public policy. Over the past three years, I have been coordinating these regular surveys, which have included questions about the economic implications of the pandemic, climate change and the Ukraine war, as well as more traditional economic concerns with jobs, inflation, competition and taxes.
- #WhatEconomistsReallyDo is an informal initiative to address common and ill-informed misperceptions of what economics is about (often published in *The Guardian* newspaper). The hashtag was coined by Oriana Bandiera at LSE and formed the title of her 2018 RES annual public lecture for school students. In a piece written with colleagues, she notes:

> all the bashing of economics can change how policy is made. It gives politicians freedom to make policy choices without being accountable to the facts. We are heading away from evidence-based policy and dangerously close to surrender to special interest groups, gut feelings and superstitions. Now, that is something truly scary.
>
> *(Bandiera et al., 2017)*

As Oriana's conclusion suggests, communicating economics to audiences beyond the ivory tower has never been more vital for public policy and public debate. What's more, as I hope this article has shown, never have there been more opportunities to reach those wider readerships. Individual economists like those mentioned here have played key roles in driving greater emphasis on effective communication of economic research analysis and evidence – but more needs to happen collectively within the profession. As demand for economic expertise rises, we need to boost the supply of public-facing economists.

Digging Deeper

Discussion Questions

1. Where do you find information about economics in the public domain?
2. How could this information be improved and spread more widely?

Suggested Further Reading

Babe, R. E. (2018) *Communication and the transformation of economics: Essays in information, public policy, and political economy*, Routledge.

References

Baldwin, R. (30 June 2017) Vox is ten years old this month, *Centre for Economic Policy Research*, https://cepr.org/voxeu/columns/vox-ten-years-old-month. Accessed 31/5/2022.

Baldwin, R. (3 April 2020) With content across the world of economics, *Centre for Economic Policy Research*, https://cepr.org/voxeu/columns/content-across-world-economics. Accessed 31/5/2022.

Bandiera, O., Attanasio, O. Blundell, R., Machin, S., Griffith, R. and Rasul, I. (20 December 2017) Dismal ignorance of the "dismal science"—a response to Larry Elliot, *Prospect,* https://www.prospectmagazine.co.uk/economics-and-finance/dismal-ignorance-of-the-dismal-science-a-response-to-larry-elliot. Accessed 31/5/2022.

Carlin, W. (2014) Wendy Carlin interviewed by Viv Davis. (20 May 2014), Teaching economics as if the last three decades had happened, *Centre for Economic Policy Research*, https://cepr.org/multimedia/teaching-economics-if-last-three-decades-had-happened. Accessed 31/5/2022.

Cecchetti, S. (2007) Federal Reserve policy actions in August 2007: frequently asked questions, VoxEU.org, 15 August, http://voxeu.org/article/subprime-crisis-faqs-revised-updated, *Economics Observatory, 2022, Economics and the Coronavirus Crisis*, https://www.economicsobservatory.com/about. Accessed 31/5/2022.

ING-Economics Network (November 2019) ING-Economics Network Survey of Public Understanding of Economics 2019, *Economics Network*, https://www.economics-network.ac.uk/research/understandingecon/2019. Accessed 31/5/2022.

Middleton, R. (1998) *Charlatans or Saviours? Economists and the British economy rom Marshall to Meade*, Edward Elgar Publishing.

Personal Correspondence (2006). For more see https://www.lse.ac.uk/marshall-institute/people/jlegrand.

Vaitilingam, R. (2020) How to write a press release, *Communicating Economics*, https://www.communicatingeconomics.com/resources/how-write-press-release. Accessed 31/5/2022.

5

HOW THE ECONOMY MUSEUM MAKES ECONOMIC PUBLIC

Thomas Shepherd and Eva Johnston

Introduction/History[1]

Thought provoking. Inspiring. An experience that can blow you away! That is the impression a Federal Reserve Bank of St. Louis employee had while visiting the Interactive Museum of Economics in Mexico City in 2008. The employee returned home with the idea of replicating the experience—incorporating hands-on activities that allow visitors to go "inside the economy" to learn how it works. This is what you'll find in the Economy Museum of the Federal Reserve Bank of St. Louis, a place where children and adults can learn by taking self-guided tours at their own pace.

The Economy Museum focuses on learning. It's a place where school groups and the public can learn about the economy, the Federal Reserve and money. When creating the museum, the Bank's content team asked a simple question: What new knowledge should visitors leave the museum with? The group easily agreed that visitors should leave knowing that they play an important role in the economy and that the decisions they make each day matter. A key concept of the museum is learning by doing. This approach helps visitors understand that economics is part of their everyday lives.

The Economy Museum at the St. Louis Fed opened in September 2014. Although the museum pays homage to history and tells the story of the Fed, the emphasis of the exhibits is on teaching visitors about the economy and their role in it.

The Exhibits—Design

At its core, the museum is a hands-on, high-tech economics lesson. It is grounded in economic definitions and employs real-world examples to illustrate the content

DOI: 10.4324/9781003283447-8

in a way that the primary audience—students in grades 6–12—can understand and relate to.

When designing the exhibits, the team focused on the fact that the economy is not something you can touch or see in an exhibit case. Rather, the exhibits would be based on a combination of concepts where the key subject matter is one that must be experienced. It was important, therefore, to identify hands-on approaches that appeal to the senses. Offering interactives and videos would allow visitors to physically and mentally involve themselves in the learning process.

As for the museum's target audience, an important concern was their level of economic knowledge. According to research, students have little economics instruction at school. To cite a recent example, the Council for Economic Education 2020 Survey of the States reveals that economics is required in only 25 of the 50 states in the United States. Testing of economics has declined with only 38% of the states requiring a standard measure of student knowledge (Council for Economic Education, 2020). As a result, it was important to the team that students leave the museum with a better understanding of the economy. One of the first challenges was to select a theme for the design of the museum that the target audience would find fun and engaging. The team brainstormed multiple possibilities but settled on one inspired by New York City's Times Square at night.

Visitors are welcomed to the museum with a video from the St. Louis Fed's president before entering the Bank's original teller area. At this point, the lights dim, and the room is transformed with a dynamic video show that describes how individuals are part of the economy. When the video ends and the lights come up, visitors see the original bank teller windows from 1925, which serve as exhibit spaces dedicated to St. Louis Fed history. Visitors then enter exhibit space where they are surrounded by glowing exhibits, bright touchscreen monitors with scrolling tickers and oversized backlit signs headlining different topics. A steady rhythm of upbeat house music further enlivens the space.

The Exhibits—Teaching Economics

You and the Economy

The first exhibit that visitors encounter is called You and the Economy. The power and consequence of choice is readily apparent with 12 different economic activities from which to select. Visitors are sure to find something of interest including shopping, video games, and cycling. They can explore and see how each pastime leads to economic activity.

Here are a few examples within the exhibit that visitors can easily relate to from the year 2020:

- Shopping: The average American household spent $1,434 on clothes, footwear and related products (Bureau of Labor Statistics, 2021).

- Playing video games: Global mobile gaming revenue exceeded $90 billion (Global Mobile Market Report, 2021).
- Riding a bicycle: Bicycle and parts sales for the global bicycle industry added up to over.
- $8.3 billion (Sorenson, 2022).

Scarcity Exhibit

Throughout the museum, glowing oversized words signal the different topic areas. In this area, the word "scarcity" introduces the first economic definition.

The exhibit explains that scarcity is simply when there are not enough resources to produce goods and services to satisfy everyone's wants. Because of this, people must make choices.

An example geared for young visitors is the choice between a new phone and a new bike. A person has been working and saving money but only has enough to buy either the phone or the bike. Scarcity means the person must choose between the two wants.

Opportunity Cost/What Do You Want?

The next exhibit focuses on another key economic concept: Opportunity cost— the highest-valued alternative that is given up when a decision is made. Using the previous example, if the person decided to buy a new phone instead of a bike, the bike is the opportunity cost.

When the Nobel-laureate economist Milton Friedman said, "There's no such thing as a free lunch," (Friedman, 1975) he was saying that there is always a cost—an opportunity cost. Someone pays for the lunch even if there is no cost to the person offered the free lunch. By accepting a free lunch, something is given up—the time that could have been spent doing something else. And the person invited to the free lunch may be obligated to something in the future.

There are more examples of opportunity cost in the exhibit called What Do You Want? After selecting the age of the visitor to provide the most accurate decision-making scenario, the visitor is presented with two options and must choose which activity to do.

In one example, a teenager is presented with a scenario about two ways to spend a Sunday afternoon: mow a neighbour's lawn and earn $20 or go to a movie with friends and spend $10? If the decision is made to mow the lawn, the teenager earned $20 from working and retained $10 not spent on a movie ticket. So, the teenager now has $30. If the decision is going to the movie, the teen gives up earning $20 and the $10 spent on the ticket.

Visitors learn that opportunity costs are incurred with all decisions, including choices about time and money. For example, visitors are given a scenario that requires choosing between attending a friend's going-away party or keeping a commitment to volunteer at a food pantry. Whichever they choose, they give up the opportunity to do the other. Economic decision-making is a powerful tool that has broad applications beyond the financial realm.

Decision Calculator

In this interactive exhibit, visitors learn that the decisions they make affect how much money is in their savings accounts or how much debt they have in the future.

A popular part of the exhibit is the Buying a Car Calculator. The first step is selecting the type of automobile to buy. Preference comes into play here. Visitors select from economy, mid-sized or luxury automobiles. The next step is to adjust factors like the loan interest rate and the length of the loan. Visitors watch the numbers change right before their eyes and see how the change impacts their monthly payment as well as the overall price they would pay for the vehicle. They walk away better prepared to make choices about an auto purchase. Seeing how the interest charged on the loan increases the final price of the car is often an eye-opener for young people. The exhibit also explains that the interest rate buyers pay is determined, in part, by their credit history.

The Trading Pit

The Trading Pit, an eight-player competitive trading game, simulates a real-time market trading experience in which players learn how markets work and gain a better understanding of how prices in competitive markets converge at market equilibrium. They learn that the interaction of buyers and sellers results in the equilibrium price in the market.

This fast-paced game features four buyers and four sellers buying and selling wheat, a common commodity in the region. All players make offers at a suggested reservation price that changes after each transaction. As the game moves along, real-time transaction information is displayed on a large, shared screen showing the price of each transaction. After a 90-second round simulating one trading day, players receive a market recap that includes which players made or lost money and which player completed the most transactions. These data points from the round inform players and allow them to make better decisions in subsequent rounds as they push toward the market-clearing price.

During their transactions over several rounds, as prices move toward competitive equilibrium, players come to understand that their individual buying and selling decisions determine prices.

Why Do We Trade?

This exhibit introduces the basic concept of trade by providing real examples of trades people make in their everyday lives. While some people only think of a trade as giving up one item for another, it is important for visitors to realize that people engage in trade to make themselves better off. Visitors who earlier decided to mow a neighbour's lawn were indeed engaged in trade with the neighbour. Mowing the lawn meant giving up time, but in return, money was earned. Other examples include trading an apple for a bag of chips while having lunch with friends.

Spice of Life Exhibit

As this popular exhibit shows, people can also learn about trade by arousing their sense of smell. Visitors read descriptions of commonly traded spices and foods. They then guess the item before flipping a panel to reveal the answer. Is the item cracked black pepper, bananas, chocolate, or pineapples? Essential oils provide the aromas and transport visitors to places where the desired products originated.

Bartering Exhibit

Barter occurs when people exchange goods and services for other goods and services without using money. People barter things that they value less to obtain things that they value more. The Barter Exhibit features an exceptional example of a real-life bartering success story. It's based on a man named Steve Ortiz, who started by trading away an old cell phone. After making 14 trades of increasing value, he ended up with a Porsche convertible. While this is an extremely unusual example, it sparks visitors' interest.

Next, visitors can try their hand at bartering by spinning wheels displaying different objects to see where barter selections can lead them. Visitors spin and select an inexpensive item such as an umbrella or ice cream cone and attempt to barter for an item of higher value. It will take several trades but the visitor can get to an item such as a television or a laptop computer. Adding a real-life element to the interactive, not all trades will be successful, and visitors might not get the item they want, assuming they want any of the choices in the end. That's one of the key takeaways with barter: For a trade to happen, both people must want what the other has. This and other challenges with bartering make getting what people want through the barter system difficult and time consuming.

Earth at Night

This exhibit features a stunning photo of the Earth's city lights at night. It was created from NASA's system designed to track clouds by moonlight as well as permanent lights on the Earth's surface. Visitors learn that the brightest areas of the Earth are those most developed and urbanized, not necessarily the most populated. Infrastructure projects, such as highways and railways connecting communities using electricity, are showcased in the picture of the Earth at night. The electricity used makes them sparkle at night around the globe.

Museum staff frequently ask visitors if they notice anything unique in the photo. It is exciting to share the fun fact that the brightly illuminated Nile River is home to 95% of Egypt's population or that lines of light that stretch across Russia are from towns along the Trans-Siberian Railway.

Standards of Living

As was seen in the Earth at Night photo, the amount of light emanating from regions around the world differ from one another.

The Standards of Living exhibit allows visitors to look at different places around the world in more detail. Comparing like things gives visitors an opportunity to evaluate standards of living. Photos of how people travel, the food they commonly eat and what school classrooms look like in different regions around the world give visitors a glimpse of how other people live. Whether transportation is via a rickshaw, reed boat, or high-speed train, seeing the variety shows different standards of living throughout the world.

The Gold Bar

The glitter of gold has allure, and the gold bar exhibit is a new exhibit that challenges people to lift a real gold bar. Visitors can reach into a secured case and attempt to lift a 28-pound gold bar. Besides being a fun experience and a great photo opportunity, the exhibit demonstrates and explains why the United States is no longer on the gold standard. Gold bars fail the portable and easily divisible tests for what makes something useful as money. The exhibit provides an explanation of the fiat currency system used today and shows where gold in the United States is stored.

Currency Exhibits

How can money be described? It's a medium of exchange, a store of value and a unit of account. Throughout the newest area of the museum, known as The Vault, visitors see colourful bills from around the world, learn about features that help to prevent counterfeiting, and get to use touchscreens tracing the history and evolution of items used for money. Visitors can also create their own currency. They can snap a photo of themselves using the available camera and select other design features to make their own unique currency in a few seconds and then receive it via email. It is a great way to make a souvenir. For those with artistic flare, paper, and drawing pencils are also available to make their own currency to take home.

Interactive Classroom Programmes

The museum staff offer a series of classroom programmes for school groups visiting the museum as well as guided questions for students to complete as they take their tour. Programme topics include:

- How the development of human capital through education and training impacts a person's income level, earning potential and unemployment
- A game show–style lesson that looks at inflation through the prices of common items over time
- An escape room–style programme that challenges students with puzzles about personal finance, money, and the Federal Reserve
- A CPI market basket lesson in which students explore a market basket of goods and services and determine what is in each category in the market basket

Every day, people participate in the economy through their daily interactions. The mission of the St. Louis Fed's Economy Museum is to simply explain how those interactions relate directly to economic concepts and provide visitors with a place where they can have fun while recognizing that *they* are the economy.

Challenges in Creating a Museum about Economics

Scarcity, a basic economic problem most people face, posed a challenge for the team. Which concepts should be included? For example, supply and demand are huge fundamental concepts. Because museum space is limited, the team chose to use the trading pit market simulation to present supply, demand and price together in the marketplace. Crafting exhibits with data about real-life experiences that incorporate more than one concept maximizes space.

Another challenge was meeting the public's expectations. When people think of a bank, they generally think of money first—not an economics lesson. While money is one facet of the economy, the team also wanted visitors to understand how developing skills and increasing human capital can allow one to earn more money. By interacting with exhibits that ask them to select an automobile or engage in trade, visitors are then able to understand how money moves through the economy.

One final ongoing challenge is explaining how the Federal Reserve System is structured and what it does and does not do. The nickname "the Fed" leads the public to assume that both the Board of Governors and the Reserve banks are directly part of the federal government. The Board of Governors, located in Washington, D.C., is in fact a federal government agency. It consists of seven members who are appointed by the president of the United States and confirmed by the Senate. These governors guide the Federal Reserve's policy actions. The Reserve banks operate somewhat independently but under the general oversight of the

Board of Governors. These Reserve banks, and their branches, are strategically located in large cities across the country. The presidents, the economists, and other employees in each of the 12 Federal Reserve districts work together to provide a regional perspective and expert knowledge about their local economies.

Digging Deeper

Discussion Questions

1. What would you design if you were asked to make an economics exhibit for a museum where you live?
2. How would you make a concept like scarcity into an interactive display?

Suggested Further Reading

Massarani, L., Rocha, J. N., Poenaru, L. M., Bravo, M., Singer, S., & Sánchez, E. (2020). La mirada de los adolescentes en una visita al Museo Interactivo de Economía (MIDE), México. *Revista Iberoamericana de Ciencia, Tecnología y Sociedad-CTS*, 15(44), 173–195.

Website of the Interactive Museum of Economics, in Mexico City: www.mide.org.mx.

Note

1 The authors would like to thank Mary C. Suiter, Ph.D., Assistant Vice President and Economic Education Officer, Federal Reserve Bank of St. Louis and Steve Greene, Assistant Vice President of Employee Communications, Federal Reserve Bank of St. Louis for editorial assistance and other support.

References

Bureau of Labor Statistics (2021). *Consumer Expenditures in 2020.* https://www.bls.gov/opub/reports/consumer-expenditures/2020/home.htm.

Council for Economic Education (2020). *Survey of the States: Economic and Personal Finance Education in Our Nation's Schools.* https://www.councilforeconed.org/wp-content/uploads/2022/03/2022-SURVEY-OF-THE-STATES.pdf.

Friedman, M. (1975). *There's No Such Thing as a Free Lunch.* Open Court.

Global Mobile Market Report (2021). Newzoo. https://newzoo.com/insights/articles/2021s-mobile-market-almost-four-billion-smartphone-users-90-7-billion-in-game-revenues-huge-changes-to-come.

Sorenson, D. (2022). *Four Ways the Cycling Industry Can Set Its Sights on Success.* The NPD Group. https://www.npd.com/news/blog/2022/four-ways-the-cycling-industry-can-set-its-sights-on-success/.

6

THE NETWORKS OF ECONOMICS

Economics About the Public Should Be for the Public

The Rethinking Economics Team

Economics about the Public Should Be for the Public

> If economists wished to study the horse, they wouldn't go and look at horses. They'd sit in their studies and say to themselves, "What would I do if I were a horse?"
>
> *Ronald Coase (cited in Earle et al., 2016, p. 41)*

Economics, both the study of economics and the formation of economic theory and policy should not just be about society but for society. The Rethinking Economics network was formed in 2014 in the wake of the 2008 financial crisis. Many of us had grown up watching our economies come crashing down around our ears and decided to study in the hope that we could better understand what had happened and be part of future solutions for more resilient national and international structures. We were bitterly disappointed to find that even though the world had changed, the textbooks hadn't.

Rather than debating and solving contemporary real-world economic challenges, we worked primarily with hypothetical examples derived from 'first principles' (assumptions that underline mainstream economic theory that are deemed to be logically sound or self-evident) that taught students how to maximise efficiency or consumers' individual utility. Case studies were scarce, and alternative economic perspectives were excluded from classroom discussions. When we tried to question why only efficiency was considered a worthy goal of economic theories, and never sustainability, gender equality or well-being, we were told that we could learn those theories in our own time but that it wasn't 'proper economics'. When we questioned why environmental limitations weren't included in resource-based models, or why we never assessed the impact of a policy on

DOI: 10.4324/9781003283447-9

gender inequality, for example, we were told that this was the remit of sociology or politics – and the goal of economics was to identify the most efficient system.

Economics is also taught from one perspective as if it is the only legitimate way to study the economy. Neoclassical economics is the dominant school of thought in the vast majority of university departments, textbooks and economics journals. It is taught without challenge and presented as a value-free science. Alternative goals for the maximisation of utility and efficiency are not considered. The result is that economics graduates are ill equipped to deal with the most pressing problems of our time – climate change, inequality, racial discrimination, global health crises and the point at which all of these challenges intersect.

Rethinking Economics calls for an economics discipline that is diverse in its approach to economic problem solving, diverse in its practitioners, encourages critical thinking, is decolonised in its mindset and is relevant to real-world problems.

In order for this to happen two things need to change. Economists must turn towards the people they are supposed to serve, and the discipline must diversify.

To understand why this change is vital, we first have to understand the game of economic policy – who makes the rules and how and what does this mean for the ways people can interact with their varied economic resources.

Rules of the Game

The way we interact with resources is governed by a number of things.

- Needs and wants – do I need to ask my friend for cooking lessons or do I want to spend my time doing something else?
- Financial access – do I have enough money to buy a car or can I only afford a bicycle?
- Power – if I demand a pay rise, will my boss have to give it to me?
- Local availability – does my local supermarket sell fresh mangoes?

The list goes on, but the one I am going to address is economic policy. The economic policy effectively sets the rules of the game. Governments set the level of taxation, import and export tariffs, the base interest rate, labour market laws, strike up trade deals with other nations, invest in infrastructure and deliver employment programmes. Sometimes international bodies like the European Union set economic policy for a group of countries. Sometimes other international bodies like the World Trade Organization recommend certain policies that countries then take up, in certain circumstances these policies are a condition for financial aid.

All of these policies impact the level of resources available in an economy, the price at which people are able to access them and the ability of individuals and communities to access certain resources (both positively and negatively). Since we all need resources, it is people and communities then who are impacted by these policies, people living in an economy are the 'end users' of economic policy.

So how does economics (as a discipline) come into this? The economics that we find in classrooms, textbooks and academic journals has a huge influence over how economic policy turns out.

Politicians and legislators have the final say on what becomes economic policy and what does not. But the content of economic policy is hugely influenced by the thinking, research and recommendations that come from university economics departments. Students of economics who don't stay in academia often graduate into the corridors of power and become government economists, ministers, journalists, bankers, civil servants and political advisors. The policies they form are based on the understanding of the economy that they have forged in their university classrooms. Economic practitioners who come to the field from outside of academic economics look to the research and thinking being produced by university economics departments, top-rated journals and leading lights in the field for guidance.

If the economic policy is the fruit, economic thinking is the tree that bears that fruit. Economists are the gardeners who sow the seeds as well as tend to the branches as the tree grows (Raworth, 2017). But the problem is, economics as a discipline is markedly cut off from the impact of the policies that are crafted in its name; the gardeners have nothing to do with the people eating the fruit. Whilst on the ground research is increasing, the theories that underpin this research are written in isolation of the economies and the economic actors they supposedly pertain to.

British economist Ronald Coase once stated, "If economists wished to study the horse, they wouldn't go and look at horses. They'd sit in their studies and say to themselves, 'What would I do if I were a horse?'". A well-known example of this is the hotly debated theory that introducing a minimum wage would increase unemployment. It's a theory you learn early on in your labour economics module and one that has been used countless times to argue against the minimum wage. This theory was considered largely uncontroversial amongst economists (who according to a survey by the American Economics Association have an average salary of $104,000 per year). A nice and neat graph could be drawn up by first-year economics students that demonstrated clearly and logically higher wages = fewer jobs. Over the last three decades, the evidence against this has been mounting. But why wasn't this theory accompanied in our textbooks by research in the first place? Quantitative research can be difficult in economics – sometimes a policy hasn't been implemented yet or been in place for long enough to test, and often there are so many other factors at play in our economies it is nearly impossible to measure the impact of a single policy on the behaviour of economic actors. But qualitative research, or at least dialogue, is much more accessible to researchers and theorists. In a meeting on decolonising economics, researchers suggested a curriculum model wherein students should meet the relevant economic actors for the topics they are studying. When studying unemployment, speak to the unemployed; when studying wage theory, speak to employers who set wages, when studying the sustainable development goals speak to companies who are meeting them, and companies who aren't. It will quickly become apparent that a one size fits all approach peddled by our economics textbooks is outdated and irrelevant for many of our local contexts.

The result of the 'graph first, research later' approach is that citizens, as the end users of economic policy are on the outside looking in. Economists sit in their ivory towers and make rules without genuine connections to the people that their policies are impacting.

Turning towards the Community

Economists need to come out of their ivory towers and build genuine connections with the end users of their policies. Rather than theorising about a 'representative agent' or discussing human behaviour from afar, citizens and consumers should be informed participants and their unique understanding of their local situation should be held in high esteem. A stark example of where this is exactly not the case is Randomised Control Trials (RCTs), which have long been used in health care but are growing increasingly popular in economics.

What is an RCT? An article by Seán Mfundza Muller, Grieve Chelwa and Nimi Hoffmann, published in *The Conversation* outlines it as

> These experiments randomly allocate a treatment to some members of a group and compare the outcomes against the other members who did not receive treatment. For example, to test whether providing credit helps to grow small firms or increase their likelihood of success, a researcher might partner with a financial institution and randomly allocate credit to applicants that meet certain basic requirements. Then a year later the researcher would compare changes in sales or employment in small firms that received the credit to those that did not.

In 2019 the Nobel Memorial Prize in Economic Sciences was awarded to Abhijit Banerjee, Esther Duflo and Michael Kremer, for their work in using RCTs in the pursuit of ending global poverty. It is in development economics and policies concerning poverty alleviation that RCTs have become most popular.

According to Muller, Chelwa and Hoffman, there are some methodological issues with RCTs that mean they rarely provide the clean control group that they intend to but also a number of ethical issues not least of which that they use citizens as guinea pigs and often fail to achieve informed consent. When public services such as schools or hospitals, it can be almost impossible for participants to opt out. And as these experiments are often conducted in impoverished communities there is a real risk for harm and exploitation, one that does not come with accountability for the economists conducting the experiment. In a piece in Promarket Ankur Sarin gives a great overview of an experiment by

Breza, Krishnaswamy and Kaur, 2016, which involved offering certain workers in Odisha (a state that is one of the poorest in India) only 75% of the legal minimum wage to test worker solidarity. Sarin asks "Why should such activity not be deemed illegal? And if it is, what legal and ethical frameworks allow researchers trained and working in the best universities of the world, to break the law with such impunity?" more questions are raised around the well-being of the participants in the survey – what happened to them after accepting wages deemed to be too low by the community? Were they ever compensated for illegally low wages? Did the researchers take responsibility for the consequences of the experiment? Whilst not every study will cause such obvious harm, it is problematic that vulnerable communities can be used to satisfy western academic interests with seemingly little accountability.

Instead of simply using people as unwitting test subjects, economists should consult and communicate. Conversations between communities, academics and policy makers that treat citizens as equal partners should be a priority both in research but also education. When learning about employment theory, students should discuss ideas with workers and employers as well as our lecturers. When studying import tariffs on basic food stuffs, we should hear from growers and consumers as well as researchers.

Rethinking Economics is building a movement for exactly these kinds of reforms to our curriculum. Whilst campaigning for a plurality of approaches to economics to be introduced to our curricula we have always been committed to being the change we want to see. These conversations do not yet take place in our classrooms, but RE student groups across the world organise workshops, discussion groups, educational events and festivals that do exactly this.

Practitioners of Economics Must Diversify in Order to Fully Represent the Communities They Serve

Our global community is diverse, but our academic community is not. The barriers to entry are high, particularly for women, people of colour, working class people, LGBT+ people, people with disabilities, people with caring responsibilities and people from the global south. It is no surprise that the supposedly 'representative agent', the theoretical prototypical person that many mainstream economists base their ideas on faces no barriers to entry of any kind. The much derided '*Homo economicus*' (Latin for 'economic man') is a perfectly rational being, who has the ability to enter into any economic transaction that he pleases. Being perfectly rational, and having all the information he needs at his disposal, he always makes the correct decision to maximise his well-being. He never gets ill, has no caring responsibilities, is never a victim of racism, sexism or ableism and seemingly never runs out of cash.

Most of us won't recognise this man, and his experience certainly won't be relatable to the vast majority of people. Yet for many economists, *Homo economicus* is the best example of how the average human behaves in any given scenario.

And therein lies the issue, there is no such thing as an 'average human'. We all have a unique set of circumstances that shapes the way we see the world and the way we behave as citizens, consumers and members of society. So why do economists act as though the 'average human' exists?

As far as academic economics goes, women, people of colour, working class people, LGBT+ people, people with disabilities, people with caring responsibilities and people from the global south are significantly underrepresented, and this continues as students and scholars move up the career ladder or into policy making. Women, for example, represent only a quarter of economists worldwide (Ambler et al., p. 25), and in the wake of the #MeToo and Black Lives Matter movements, increasingly reports are surfacing of these old, white and male environments being actively hostile to people from these groups who manage to break through.

The effect of the discipline being divorced from many people's lived reality is compounded by the lack of diversity amongst thinkers at the table. Economics produces theories, policies and research which ignore marginalised groups, disparities between races, genders and people of different social classes are invisible in neoclassical models. The theories and case studies that we learn are overwhelmingly Eurocentric and the role of the slave trade in the economic growth associated with the Industrial Revolution is repeatedly ignored.

Furthermore, by excluding diverse voices, we undermine democratic development (Ambler et al., 2022, pp. 161–200). What is considered a 'developed' economy is largely modelled on western nations that became rich off the back of the industrial revolution. But the policies that are recommended for the 'less developed' world to 'catch up' are not necessarily those that proved effective in the western industrial revolution but rather those that that fit within a neoclassical framework and are considered 'beneficial' to international trade (Chang, 2002). Beneficial to whom exactly, is a question rarely raised in classroom or policy discussions because there is an unspoken understanding amongst the people in the room that it is beneficial to them. By facilitating conversations between diverse practitioners we create space for these questions to arise.

Citizens from across social groups, identities and geographical locations should not be *just* end users of economic policy but also thought leaders and consultants in the formation of it so that what is put into practice is a true reflection of their priorities and values. Rethinking Economics campaigns to highlight the lack of diversity in economics and for students and scholars to decolonise their thinking. It is essential that we increase representation for currently marginalised groups, because with increased diversity the necessary decolonisation of our practices, theories and mindsets is inevitable.

Our Economies Must Serve People and the Planet

Rethinking Economics is a movement that exists across the world to change economics from the ground up, we organise in two ways:

1. We form groups at universities who organise self-education events and lobby their economics department to reform the curriculum

2. We build a global network of critical economists, who will graduate into academia, economic institutions, finance and policy making and be the change we want to see

Why? Our economies need to serve people and the planet we inhabit. For this to happen the guardians of our economies, that is economists, must see themselves in the service of global citizens. And it is as guardians of our economies, rather than technocrats or social scientists, that they should build theories, policies and narratives around the discipline of economics. For our economies to truly serve the public, our economists must first recognise the crucial role that the economics discipline and that economists play in shaping our social & economic lives. Economics will not succeed in serving our global community however, until it begins to accurately represent it. The field of economics must diversify and our thinking must decolonise. When a range of voices are amplified, only then can economics become a thriving forum of innovation and new ideas that functions for the benefit of us all.

How We Are Rethinking Economics

Economic knowledge production and policy making have been relegated to the realm of a small group of certified experts. In this environment, basic economic concepts are often mystified and made unnecessarily inaccessible to a wider public. Democratising economic knowledge is a key first step in expanding public participation in economic decisions, which is essential to democracy. Rethinking Economics works with our students to provide economics explainer courses to children aged 14–18 to help unpack economic terms and provide alternative perspectives on real-world issues.

We make economics public through our yearly conferences. As a network of 130 groups in over 30 countries, there are several in-person and online conferences and courses held every year under the banner of Rethinking Economics. Our digital conference in 2021 aimed to unpack real-world issues that students cared about and offer debates and talks about how best to tackle them with alternative economic thinking. Our network produces thousands of rethinkers each year looking to change the face of the economist from one that serves the community, instead of extracting from it.

Digging Deeper

Discussion Questions

1. How do you imagine a stereotypical economist?
2. In what ways having a diversity workforce in economics might change what economics does?

Suggested Further Reading

Earle, J., Moran, C., & Ward-Perkins, Z. (2016). *The Econocracy: the perils of leaving economics to the experts.* Manchester University Press.

References

Ambler, L., Earle, J., & Scott, N. (2022). *Reclaiming economics for future generations.* Manchester: Manchester University Press. http://www.jstor.org/stable/j.ctv29mvt6p.

Chang, H. J. (2002). *Kicking away the ladder: development strategy in historical perspective.* London and New York: Anthem Press.

Earle, J., Moran, C., & Ward-Perkins, Z. (2016). *The Econocracy: the perils of leaving economics to the experts.* Manchester: Manchester University Press.

Muller, S. M., Chelwa, G., Hoffmann, N. (2019). 'How Randomised Trials Became Big in Development Economics.' The Conversation. https://theconversation.com/how-randomised-trials-became-big-in-development-economics-128398, December 9.

Perry, K. (2020). Rethink Economics to Help Marginalized People. *Nature, 582*(7812), 341–342.

Raworth, K. (2017). *Doughnut economics: seven ways to think like a 21st-century economist.* White River Junction, VT: Chelsea Green Publishing.

Sarin, A. (2020). 'Indecent Proposals in Economics: The Moral Problem with Randomized Trial Experiments.' ProMarket. https://promarket.org/2020/05/21/indecent-proposals-in-economics-the-moral-problem-with-randomized-trial-experiments/, May 21.

The Economist Intelligence Unit (2020). 'What Harm Do Minimum Wages Do?' *The Economist.* https://www.economist.com/schools-brief/2020/08/15/what-harm-do-minimum-wages-do, August 15.

7

MORE TALK, LESS CHALK

Communicating Economics in the Modern Classroom[1]

Christopher L. Colvin

There is something of a paradox in university-level economics teaching. Economics graduates continue to achieve extremely good labour market outcomes.[2] But for over a decade now students and graduate employers have voiced concerns that the contents of economics degrees are "out of touch".[3] The mixture of transferable skills and quantitative methods taught in undergraduate economics programmes helps to explain the former. The dominance of de-contextualised mathematical economics teaching is no doubt one cause of the latter. Mathematics is a valuable skill that teaches students to construct logical arguments and think in abstract ways. But mathematics is just one of the many languages of economics; if economics students wish to persuade their audiences and make a useful contribution, then they must also learn to communicate their ideas in words.

Course outlines and programme specifications typically list "communication skills" among the expected learning outcomes of economics degrees. But these skills are almost never addressed formally. Rather, students are expected to gain them by participating in formative classroom activities or completing their summative assessments. I think students additionally benefit from taking a dedicated communication course. At Queen's University Belfast, I had the opportunity to create just such a course as part of a restructuring of our first-year undergraduate curriculum. My course, titled *Communicating Economics*, now sits alongside *Principles of Economics* and *Mathematics for Economists* as a compulsory component of the first semester of our three-year single-honours BSc Economics degree.[4]

My aim was to design a course that would help students become "well-rounded" economists by helping them to better articulate their ideas in words. I wished to intervene early, right at the start of their academic journey, rather than bolt on communication skills to the end of their third year of study. The way I teach economic communication is by stimulating students to think about what

DOI: 10.4324/9781003283447-10

economics as a discipline is trying to achieve, and exposing them to the myriad ways in which economists attempt to persuade. This requires me to discuss more conceptual material from economic methodology, philosophy and rhetoric. Students learn how the communication of economic ideas is driven by context. The "real-world" applications I use give students a chance to "use" economics in problem-solving contexts – something absent from the first year of a traditional UK economics degree. I hope my selection of economics topics also exposes students to some important, controversial societal questions where economics, when communicated well, can prove useful.

Course Description

My *Communicating Economics* course has five interlinked units, each of which approaches economics through a different lens. Each unit comes in two parts: a more conceptual treatment of the topic; and an applied class where I make use of these concepts to explain some economic phenomena – here they learn some new economics along the way. My five units are: (1) economics as science, (2) economics as literature, (3) economics as politics, (4) economics as history and (5) economics as philosophy. I introduce each below, before sketching the second topic in more detail in the sections that follow.

1. Economics is science in that it deals in causal relationships, relies on measurement and metrics and purports to be inherently falsifiable. Like other sciences, economists move between abstract theory and real-world evidence to build their analyses and prescribe their policy initiatives. Scientific language is integral to the way economists communicate. The "scientific lens" is typically the sole perspective through which economics is presented in principles textbooks. This unit introduces students to how economists use scientific language when they attempt to persuade their audiences and lays the foundations for subsequent comparisons with other approaches to economic communication. My application is to the economics of climate change, where we focus on the societal function of climate modelling.

2. Economics is literature in that it can have intrinsic artistic or intellectual value aside from its intended practical function of understanding the economy. But more fundamentally, economists share the art of storytelling with novelists, playwrights and scriptwriters as a method of communicating their ideas. The aim of this unit is to introduce to students the idea of economics as storytelling, to equip them with the skills to identify and reflect upon popular recurring economic stories, and then to encourage them to write their own versions of these economic stories. I apply these ideas to look at the economics of science fiction, which builds on economic ideas and contexts from fields such as business economics, environmental economics and political economy.

3.   Economics is politics in that it is used to inform government policy decisions and justify partisan communications. Economists have fostered a schism and developed an associated language, to keep positive ("what is") and normative ("what should be") economic insights distinct and separate. But this distinction does not always work very well, which provides great material for classroom discussion. This unit concerns the ways politicians and public intellectuals use, but also abuse, economics to persuade their audiences. This unit allows me to re-consider the use of economics in the Brexit referendum campaign as my application.

4.   Economics is history in two distinct ways: economic evidence is historical by definition and benefits from historical methods to assess its reliability and relevance; and historical events and processes help to explain many present-day economic phenomena. This topic focuses on the ways in which the discipline of economic history can have a useful influence on economics and economists. The contrasting ways in which economists and historians communicate their views is a particular focus; to put it crudely, economists are typically concerned with averages and aggregates, while historians are with contingency and outliers. My application for this unit is to put Covid-19 public health policy in an historical context and think about learning from past pandemics.

Finally, then, (5) economics is philosophy in that it deals with fundamental questions of existence, knowledge, values, reason, mind and language. This topic links together some of the key insights from across the course with more formal ideas from the philosophy of science to better understand economic rhetoric. I also discuss some core assumptions made in mainstream economic modelling in light of ideas from moral philosophy. Indeed, as the application in this unit, I get students to read and translate extracts from Adam Smith's *Wealth of Nations* (1776) about the concept of natural justice.

Narrative Storytelling in Economics

The "Economics as Literature" unit, like the others in my *Communicating Economics* course, comes in two parts: a more conceptual treatment of the topic; and an applied class where I make use of these concepts to describe and explain a set of economic phenomena. My conceptual lecture focuses mainly on introducing students to the ideas of four "Big Thinkers" who have engaged with economic storytelling in their own work, but in quite different ways: Deirdre McCloskey, Mary Morgan, Avner Greif and Robert Shiller. The application class, which follows immediately in the sequence, applies these ideas to the science fiction literary genre, focusing on the economic stories of some famous – and some less famous – futuristic fiction franchises.

The unit is then accompanied by two small-group discussion classes across two consecutive weeks, in which students prepare activities that reinforce their learning. Here I force students to identify and retell economic stories by completing two activities: composing haiku, a short form of poetry from Japan (following Ziliak, 2009), and narrating old episodes of *The Simpsons*, a popular animated sitcom from the US (following Hall, 2014). Finally, the assessment of this part of the course relies on keeping a regular reflective reading journal, where students retell and criticise major current economic stories that they read across different media outlets. I explain all these teaching settings in what follows, starting with the conceptual lecture.

Insights from the work of Deirdre McCloskey form the starting point of this unit. In a series of contributions on rhetoric – "the art of persuasion" – she argues that economics is as much a literary discipline as a scientific one.[5] Paraphrasing McCloskey's argument: like novelists, economists have two modes of explanation: we make use of stories and metaphors. She defines "stories" as backward-looking explanatory narratives, while "metaphors" are more like our forward-looking abstract predictive models. Economists use these modes in different contexts, for different purposes, and their use can come into conflict. Making a distinction like McCloskey's is important because it helps students to understand how economists systematise and rationalise the world around them, and then how they attempt to communicate their knowledge to others. I am convinced making students more self-aware helps them to better communicate their own ideas.

The stories/metaphors dichotomy should then help students to make deeper realisations about the nature of economic knowledge: understanding why economists disagree about practically everything. Because points of disagreement are, according to McCloskey, not necessarily down to the things that economists usually ascribe them to, like differences in modelling assumptions or adherence to different schools of thought. Rather, they are down to the ways in which economics is communicated between economists. This involves introducing students to a richer "theory of reading" that involves reading economic texts as if they are literary prose full of complications and hidden meanings; where the compression of knowledge into prose means crucial things are left out; and where the reader is not always capable of assuming the point of view of the author.

I then apply this logic to a topic close to McCloskey's own research agenda: understanding the causes of the Industrial Revolution.[6] We discuss the competing explanations that are advanced in the literature to explain why the Industrial Revolution occurred first in Britain in the late-eighteenth century. I present a brief historiography – a history of the history-writing – to show how the explanations have changed over time. I include McCloskey's own explanations for the phenomenon and show how they have developed over the past few decades, culminating in her current explanation, which stresses the essential role of language and rhetoric in developing liberal bourgeois ideas and values.[7] Because the Industrial Revolution occurred only once, I make the point that modelling it is very difficult – but not for want of trying. Instead, economists typically make use of their storytelling mode of explanation, which stresses context, contingency and nuance.

Mary Morgan looks at the way scientists explain with statistics, models, measurements, experiments and observations. Looking at Morgan's (2017) work on "narrative science" is for me a logical next step in building students' ability to reflect on what economists attempt to achieve in their communications. Morgan describes building narratives as a process of "ordering material", which scientists achieve in a variety of different ways besides written prose – including through diagrams, flowcharts, maps and equations. She contrasts "chronicles" with "narratives", with the former being about ordering events chronologically through time, while the latter goes further by implying relationships between events. Narratives, she argues, have a question-answer or problem-solving nature. Scientific narratives differ from those written by historians in that they are less interested in the particulars, and more interested categories, concepts and theories. They may lack the time dimension of historical narratives, focusing instead on some other configuring logic. While narratives can only explain in the particular context of their usage, Morgan argues scientific narratives can "travel beyond the case" and be repeatedly reused.

After these more "meta" approaches to classifying narratives, I continue with a more tangible use of the term originating from the field of economic history: we look at "analytic narratives" as a research methodology.[8] Popularised by Avner Greif (1989) in his work on eleventh-century trade networks in the Mediterranean, this approach typically makes use of rational choice theories to fill in the gaps where the evidence is non-existent. Analytic narratives have been described by Boettke (2000) as "thick" descriptions with "dirty" data – which contrast with the "thin" descriptions provided by mathematical economics models and "clean" data used by econometricians. Applications have solved a range of economic puzzles, from describing the political economy of piracy in Leeson (2007) to explaining the spectacular failure of the DeLorean Motor Company in Brownlow (2015). This is a hybrid approach to storytelling, which mixes economics' literary and scientific lenses. Exposure to analytic narratives helps students reconcile the two, and brings them to something that is much closer to how policymakers *actually* analyse, narrate and persuade.

I end my conceptual discussion by looking at an altogether different use of the term "narrative" by an economist. Robert Shiller (2017, 2019) coins the phrase "narrative economics" to describe how stories that offer an interpretation of economic events can themselves have the power to affect collective behaviour in the economy. Rather than looking at narratives from the perspective of a linguist, Shiller reserves the term "economic narratives" for stories that "do" something. Framing his idea using simple models from epidemiology, he argues that a small number of initial propagators can influence collective behaviour as their narratives can infect society like a virus. He identifies a set of "perennial narratives" that have recurred frequently in history: from bubble narratives that affect the stock market to political narratives that affect election outcomes. Crucially, these narratives do not need to be true for them to have an economic impact; they can be self-fulfilling.

Shiller's conceptualisation of narratives and their impact will sound familiar to social scientists who study memes.[9] But I think his idea is an original contribution because he is essentially presenting a theory that McCloskey's stories (backward-looking explanatory narratives) as sometimes having a dual purpose in also constituting metaphors (forward-looking abstract predictive models). He is also offering a specific mechanism that explains how Morgan's scientific narratives are being repeatedly reused in different contexts.

Introducing Shiller's ideas in class also helps me to initiate a discussion about the way economic stories and metaphors can become "performative" – economic ideas taught in the classroom have the potential to affect how students subsequently behave.[10] My aim here is that when my first-year students are learning about downward-sloping demand curves and efficient markets in their *Principles* course, they are equipped to reflect on the fact that these are "just" models of human behaviour. They are intended to reflect reality, but they are not "real" per se – unless students make them real by internalising the models and behaving according to their predictions unless they become collective economic narratives.[11] This discussion also provides students with the necessary scepticism when evaluating Greif's use of rational choice theories in his analytic narratives.

Economics and Science Fiction

Science fiction deals with imaginative and futuristic concepts, such as advanced science and technology, time travel, parallel universes, space exploration and extra-terrestrial life. The genre provides an entertaining criticism of our present-day society. Besides John Maynard Keynes's (1930) optimistic vision of the future of society, or Paul Krugman's (2010) tongue-in-cheek treatment of interstellar trade, science fiction is something not typically associated with economics. But science fiction *is* economics. At first glance, science fiction universes are all about technology. Really, though, technology is just a side-show; the real focus is on socio-economic relations between the protagonist and the economic institutions that form the setting. I see science fiction universes as hypothetical counterfactuals; if you strip out the futuristic technologies, they are extreme scenarios where something drastic has changed the nature of society – typically the realisation of some catastrophic risk. They are a way through which stories about present-day economic problems can reach mass non-academic audiences.

If science fiction is economics, then economics is in some sense also science fiction. Indeed, this is the proposition of Ha-Joon Chang in his contribution to an excellent book of essays edited by William Davies (2018). According to Chang, the mainstream idea that economics does not involve ethical and political judgement is "downright wrong"; the positive-normative distinction "scientific" economists cling onto is artificial – it is a "science fiction". Chang also believes economics is science fiction because of a belief he thinks underpins mainstream economics: that scientific progress will solve all societal problems – essentially, we are all actors in a Whig history.

The two-way economics-science fiction relationship is the focus of my application lecture because it gets students thinking about the nature of economics, the way it is communicated to non-economists and the influence it has on our behaviour. Talking about science fiction is also fun – at least, it is for me. There exist a limited number of recurring science fiction stories that we can treat as economic narratives. My lecture takes students through three such narratives: (1) the disruptive nature of automation, (2) the problems with the corporation as a legal form for organising business and (3) the tendencies and ways in which the state can abuse its power over citizens.[12] I illustrate each with examples from science fiction. In choosing these settings, I introduce students to some important economic ideas and then give them a context in which to apply these ideas. Throughout the discussion, I get them to categorise my chosen works of science fiction using the taxonomies of McCloskey, Morgan, Greif and Shiller. Besides contributions to Davies (2018), two excellent books that have helped me plan and frame this lesson are: Saadia (2016) and Sanchez-Pages (2021).

1. Automation is one of Shiller's perennial economic narratives and one that is once again being actively discussed in the media. After defining some core terms and introducing students to the Beverage Curve, I discuss an article by Caprettini and Voth (2020) that looks at the Swing riots in England during the 1830s.[13] These riots were a response to new labour-saving technologies introduced to rural society during the Industrial Revolution. This sets us up for a discussion of James Cameron's movie *The Terminator* (1984) and its sequels. Arnold Schwarzenegger's cyborg assassin character is very literally about machines taking over and replacing humans. The future universe from which this cyborg time travels to the present has been ravaged by machines, who have enslaved mankind.[14] This movie also helps me to talk about the use of counterfactuals in economic argumentation.

2. Presenting the powerful idea of the corporation as constituting a nexus of contracts that can take transactions outside of the market and into hierarchies of control is the starting point for my second science fiction backdrop. After giving them some historical context on the emergence of the corporation as a legal form of enterprise in the Dutch Republic, I go through the core characteristics that define the modern corporation – including separate legal personality and the separation of ownership from control.[15] The latter allows me to introduce students to the principal-agent problem. My science fiction application is Ridley Scott's movie *Blade Runner* (1982), itself an adaptation of Philip K. Dick's novel *Do Androids Dream of Electric Sheep?* (1968). This noir fiction has at its centre a police investigation by Harrison Ford's android hunter Rick Deckard character. The dystopian world he inhabits is dominated by monopolistic mega-corporations, the most powerful among

which is the Tyrell Corporation, responsible for manufacturing the androids exploited for manual labour in space colonies. The Tyrell Corporation, like the Dutch East India Company, suffers from crippling corporate governance conflicts which ultimately lead to its demise.[16] The questions left intentionally unanswered by the movie – is Deckard himself a replicant? – provide examples of McCloskey's theory of reading.

3. Political economy is not something that is typically taught to first-year economics students. But I think it should be. After all, it deals with important normative economic questions: who gets what, who gets to be what, and who gets to do what. After introducing students to the contractarian relationship between the individual and the state that is typically central to mainstream economics, we discuss what makes a democratic state democratic. Already familiar with the concept of market failure, we then build on this and discuss government failure: administrative infeasibility and special interests. My science fiction application is Richard Fleischer' movie *Soylent Green* (1973), an adaptation of Harry Harrison's novel *Make Room! Make Room!* (1966), in which Charlton Heston's NYPD detective character Frank Thorn finds out that the state is converting people into foodstuff. The context here is an overpopulated world ravaged by climate catastrophe. In this story, New York's citizens have no agency; their status is dictated by the state. A wealthy elite have disproportionate access to society's remaining resources. And the populace is kept under control by making it dependent on the state for all its necessities.[17] *Soylent Green* allows me to contrast the historical narrative that focuses on the individual actors in the story, with the economic one about the configuration of the post-apocalyptic society.

Broadening Perspectives

Communicating Economics has run for three cycles here at Queen's. The second time I delivered it online because of the pandemic. Overall, students find this a challenging course but seem to enjoy it nonetheless. They are not used to thinking about the material I present; students typically have a quite narrow view of what constitutes economics when they start out, and their lens is closest to my "economics as science" unit. But after some initial hesitancy, I think I convince them that economics is a more varied and interesting discipline – that it is more than just applied mathematics.

Essentially, my course has two main aims: (1) to get students to reflect on the impact economic communication has on what economists have to say about the economy and (2) to improve their written and oral economics communication skills. It has so far proved difficult to assess whether this early intervention in their first year of study has an overall impact on student achievement later in their degree programmes; there have been many other changes these past few years making an evaluation very difficult.

Digging Deeper

Discussion Questions

1. Can you think of other examples where science fiction is really economics fiction?
2. Apart from communication skills, are there other topics missing from a basic economics education?

Suggested Further Reading

Castronova, E. (2001). *Virtual Worlds: A First-Hand Account of Market and Society on the Cyberian Frontier.* Available at SSRN 294828.
Website of Communicating Economics: www.communicatingeconomics.com.

Notes

1 I thank Duncan McVicar for support in establishing this course, Graham Brownlow and members of the Queen's Management School Teaching and Learning Forum for acting as a sounding board for ideas, and Rachel Griffith for sharing teaching material from her course at the University of Manchester.
2 See, e.g., Belfield et al. (2018), where these graduate outcomes are measured in terms of earning premia.
3 See contributions by graduate employers to Coyle (2012), and discussion of a curriculum survey in Earle et al. (2017).
4 Similar courses exist at the universities of Bristol and Manchester but are pitched as optional modules for more advanced students later in their degree. Conversations with Rachel Griffith, who teaches the course at Manchester, were particularly useful when I was designing my own course. Together with Maeve Cohen, Bob Denham and Romesh Vaitilingam, she runs an excellent pedagogical website on economics communication: https://communicatingeconomics.com/.
5 McCloskey's writings on rhetoric are extensive. I suggest readers start with McCloskey (1990, 1994), and then move on to McCloskey (1998).
6 Besides being an economic historian myself, I chose this application because some of the relevant economics appears in the *Principles* textbook we use here at Queen's: the CORE project's *The Economy*. This is an open-source online textbook, available at: www.core-econ.org/the-economy/. Units 1 and 2 concern the Industrial Revolution, and present Robert Allen's modelling thereof.
7 For a popular treatment of McCloskey's thesis, see McCloskey and Carden (2020).
8 See Koyama (2018) for an accessible review of this approach.
9 For a classic scientific study of memes, see Blackmore (1999). For a sceptical discussion about the possible emergence of a "narrative turn" in economics, see Sacco (2020).
10 Performativity in economics is normally attributed to Callon (1998). MacKenzie (2006) provides an accessible application to financial economics. Unfortunately, the meaning of the term performative in popular discourse is the precise opposite of the meaning it has here.

11 There is an active discussion about the dangers of teaching *Principles* courses without addressing performativity – what the economics blogger Noah Smith (2016) calls "101ism". There is also a literature on whether economists behave differently from others – principally, whether economists are more selfish and less trusting of others (Gerlach, 2017).

12 Unit 16 of *The Economy* covers automation; unit 6 covers the corporation; and unit 22 covers the state.

13 An accessible summary is available on the VoxEU website: https://voxeu.org/article/rage-against-machines-new-technology-and-violent-unrest.

14 There are many other science fiction works besides *The Terminator* that have this same theme, including, of course, some of the stories in Isaac Asimov's *I, Robot* (1950).

15 See Gelderblom et al. (2013) for how these characteristics first emerged in the Dutch East India Company.

16 Another great science fiction application of the corporation is the profit-driven corporate culture of the alien Ferengi Alliance in the *Star Trek* universe, designed as a counterfactual to the post-capitalist utopian Federation of Planets. I like to show students an extract of *Star Trek: Deep Space Nine* episode *Rules of Acquisition* (S2 E7, 1996).

17 Other relevant science fiction applications include George Lucas's *Star Wars* franchise, the first instalment of which first instalment of which (retroactively titled *Star Wars: Episode IV – A New Hope*) appeared in 1977, at the height of the cold war. It presents a conflict between good and evil, democracy and dictatorship. Contractarianism is central to the plot; free libertarian utopia with minimal state intervention is the goal of (some of) the movie's protagonists.

References

Asimov, I. (1950). *I, Robot*. New York: Gnome Press.

Bates, R. H., Greif, A., Levi, M., Rosenthal, J. L., & Weingast, B. R. (1998). *Analytic Narratives*. Princeton, NJ: Princeton University Press.

Belfield, C., Britton, J., Buscha, F., Dearden, L., Dickson, M., Van Der Erve, L., Sibieta, L., Vignoles, A., Walker, I., & Zhu, Y. (2018). The relative labour market returns to different degrees. Institute for Fiscal Studies for UK Department for Education, Report No. DFE-RR787 (2018).

Blackmore, S. (1999). *The Meme Machine*. Oxford: Oxford University Press.

Boettke, P. J. (2000). Review of: analytic narratives. In Bates, R. H., Greif, A., Levi, M., Rosenthal, J. L., & Weingast, B. R. (Eds.), *Constitutional Political Economy, 11*, 377–379.

Brownlow, G. (2015). Back to the failure: an analytic narrative of the De Lorean debacle. *Business History, 57*(1), 156–181.

Callon, M. (1998). *The Laws of the Markets*. Oxford: Blackwell.

Caprettini, B., & Voth, H. J. (2020). Rage against the machines: labor-saving technology and unrest in industrializing England. *American Economic Review: Insights, 2*(3), 305–320.

Chang, H. J. (2018). Economics, science fiction, history and comparative studies. In W. Davies (Ed.), *Economic Science Fictions* (pp. 31–40). London: Goldsmiths Press.

Coyle, Diane (Ed.). (2012). *What's the Use of Economics? Teaching the Dismal Science after the Crisis*. London: London Publishing Partnership.

Davies, W. (Ed.). (2018). *Economic Science Fictions*. London: Goldsmiths Press.

Dick, P. K. (1968). *Do Androids Dream of Electric Sheep?* New York: Doubleday.

Earle, J., Moran, C., & Ward-Perkins, Z. (2017). The econocracy: the perils of leaving economics to the experts. In *The Econocracy*. London: Penguin Books.

Gelderblom, O., De Jong, A., & Jonker, J. (2013). The formative years of the modern corporation: the Dutch East India Company VOC, 1602–1623. *The Journal of Economic History, 73*(4), 1050–1076.

Gerlach, P. (2017). The games economists play: why economics students behave more selfishly than other students. *PloS One, 12*(9), e0183814.

Greif, A. (1989). Reputation and coalitions in medieval trade: evidence on the Maghribi traders. *The Journal of Economic History, 49*(4), 857–882.

Hall, J. (Ed.). (2014). *Homer Economicus: The Simpsons and Economics.* Stanford, CA: Stanford University Press.

Harrison, H. (1966). *Make Room! Make Room!* New York: Doubleday.

Keynes, J. M. (1963). Economic possibilities for our grandchildren (1930). In *Essays in Persuasion*, J.M. Keynes, Ed. (pp. 358–373). New York: W.W. Norton & Co.

Koyama, M. (2018). Analytic narratives. In M. Blum, & C. L. Colvin (Eds.), *An Economist's Guide to Economic History* (pp. 371–378). Cham: Palgrave Macmillan.

Krugman, P. (2010). The theory of interstellar trade. *Economic Inquiry, 48*(4), 1119–1123.

Leeson, P. T. (2007). An-arrgh-chy: the law and economics of pirate organization. *Journal of Political Economy, 115*(6), 1049–1094.

MacKenzie, D. (2006). Is economics performative? Option theory and the construction of derivatives markets. *Journal of the History of Economic Thought, 28*(1), 29–55.

McCloskey, D. N. (1990). Storytelling in economics. In C. Nash, & M. Warner (Eds.), *Narrative in Culture* (pp. 5–22). London: Routledge.

McCloskey, D. N. (1994). How economists persuade. *Journal of Economic Methodology, 1*(1), 15–32.

McCloskey, D. N. (1998). *The Rhetoric of Economics* (2nd ed.). Madison: University of Wisconsin Press.

McCloskey, D. N., & Carden, A. (2020). *Leave Me Alone and I'll Make You Rich: How the Bourgeois Deal Enriched the World.* Chicago, IL: University of Chicago Press.

Morgan, M. S. (2017). Narrative ordering and explanation. *Studies in History and Philosophy of Science Part A, 62*, 86–97.

Saadia, M. (2016). *Trekonomics: The Economics of* Star Trek. San Francisco, CA: Inkshares.

Sacco, P. L. (2020). 'There are more things in heaven and earth…' A 'narrative turn' in economics?' *Journal of Cultural Economics, 44*, 173–183.

Sanchez-Pages, S. (2021). *The Representation of Economics in Cinema: Scarcity, Greed and Utopia.* Cham: Palgrave Macmillan.

Shiller, R. J. (2017). Narrative economics. *American Economic Review, 107*(4), 967–1004.

Shiller, R. J. (2019). *Narrative Economics: How Stories Go Viral and Drive Major Economic Events.* Princeton, NJ: Princeton University Press.

Smith, A. (1776). *An Inquiry into the Nature and Causes of the Wealth of Nations.* London: W. Strahan and T. Cadell.

Smith, N. (2016, 21 January). 101ism. *Noahpinion.* http://noahpinionblog.blogspot.com/2016/01/101ism.html.

The Core Team (2017). *The Economy.* https://www.core-econ.org/the-economy/.

Ziliak, S. T. (2009). Haiku economics: little teaching aids for big economic pluralists. *International Journal of Pluralism and Economics Education, 1*(1–2), 108–129.

SECTION THREE

Challenges in Communicating Economics

In the previous section, we have looked at the practical ways people are working – in networks, museums, media and universities – to make economics a more public discipline and set of knowledge. This is hard, but important, work.

In this section, the authors will focus on some of the challenges in making economics truly public, as a discipline and as content.

The first chapter in this section, Chapter 8, by Vicki Macknight, invites us to become aware of some of the complexities of making economics public. By looking at a mundane moment in how we interact with knowledge, sitting half-distracted with a phone, we are shown that there is also irreducible messiness to how economics actually is in the public domain. Macknight opens up the discussion of authority (who has the right to say what economics is), how to know (and what resources are we competing for in an information economy) and where the moral/ethical heart of economics is located.

These themes are taken up by the other authors in this section, who accept that it is not so easy to make economics public, and that for a variety of reasons. If we are intent on making economics more public, then we face challenges for our politics, our trust in experts and our sense of the ethical dimensions of economics.

For Kevin Albertson, the challenges are political. In particular, he argues for a contradiction at the heart of capitalist democracies. This lies in the tension between votes for all (democracy) and ownership for some (capitalist accumulation), especially when ownership comes to encompass media, think tanks and lobbyists.

Carlo Martini considers the ever-vexing problem of how to tell science from pseudo-science – and if we assume economics is a science, how to tell economics from pseudo-economics. Producing high-quality economic research is costly, he

DOI: 10.4324/9781003283447-11

points out, and yet, with such a large potential impact on policy, there are strong incentives to push narratives based on pseudo-economics. This becomes a particularly important issue for anyone who seeks to make economics more public – we must be thinking in particular about how to make good quality economics more public and how to teach people to discern the difference. Martini closes his chapter by highlighting some common red flags that mark pseudo-economics from its more reliable other.

For Joan Leach and Fabien Medvecky, a central challenge lies in the dubious (or exaggerated) dichotomy between positive and normative economics, which has enabled questions of how to communicate economics ethically to hide in plain sight. If economists pretend that there is a difference between stating 'what is' and wondering 'what matters', then the assumptions about 'what matters' can continue to lurk unquestioned within their 'what is' claims – their models, trends and so on.

Happily, each chapter also comes with suggestions about how to begin to overcome the challenges. For Alberston, a robust and civic-minded economics education would help. For Martini, paying attention to the red flags that bring pseudo-economics to our attention is important. For Leach and Medvecky, there are lessons to be learned from science communication, or more accurately, from the ethical journey that science communication has been on and continues to take.

8

KNOWING ECONOMICS WITH YOUR PHONE

Vicki Macknight

Introduction

The baby is drifting off to sleep, while I sit beside him, patting his tummy and humming tunelessly. Mothers, they say, are supposed to multi-task, and so I am. I type [economics] into my phone, a knowledge tool that is embedded in our lives and in our knowledge habits more and more, and in ways we don't often stop to think about. I want to know what people would learn about economics when this – stuck in the middle of normal life, android phone in hand – is often how they come to know.

This question is important for economics because our screens are a major way the public come to know about all sorts of things, including the discipline of economics. It matters what people think economics is, how definite and how authoritative it seems, how easy it is being made to know about it and how it is linked to worlds of money (and the economy) and education. But there is more too. There is a conflict of interest here. Google,[1] after all, is a mega corporation, its success is inextricably connected to the free-market economy (Lee, 2010) and especially an economy privileging tech entrepreneurs (Fuchs, 2012). And here they are, responsible in part for teaching people what 'economics' is (Macknight, 2020).

When we ask questions about what people know with Google, we are quickly led to thinking about algorithms and what we can and should know about them. Francis Lee and Lotta Björklund Larsen (2019) write about the ways we talk about algorithms as 'black boxes' – we don't and can't know enough about how tech companies are using algorithms to sort out what data to show us. That mystery can become an obsession, but a dead-end one. Instead, Lee and Larsen along with others (see, for example, Bucher, 2017; Ananny, 2016) have argued that what is important is not what is hidden in algorithmic operations, but what

DOI: 10.4324/9781003283447-12

is in plain sight – the results of the algorithm show us on our screens. I follow that lead, telling you about the significance of what I see, spending less time wondering why.

Google Epistemology?

Google accounts for the vast majority of online desktop searches[2] as well as 93% of mobile searches in the United States in 2021.[3] With so many people searching, what they know from Google becomes a hugely important question. But how can we learn what other people know from Google? This question gathers up problems from previous strands of epistemology, like subjectivity, perception and justification, and compounds them. The trouble is, in part, the individual tailoring of each person's information. Google's algorithms take in multiple signals about a user and vary search results accordingly. But exactly what signals, how many of them or how those signals might impact results are commercially sensitive secrets. One estimate has put the signals at 200, including location, time of day and search history (Graham, 2017, p. 40). Others have estimated many, many more.[4]

More, the hardware used to search makes a difference to what searchers are shown. Mobile and desktop search results are different, with one estimate suggesting they can be up to 79% different.[5] Google is aware of the different ways people use phones compared with desktop computers and uses a range of strategies to keep users entangled with each as an information infrastructure. It is not enough to think of ourselves as Google knowers (Macknight and Medvecky, 2020; Lynch, 2016; Gunn and Lynch, 2018) when the platform and hardware we Google search on the impacts what we are shown. This means it is more accurate, though less catchy, to think of ourselves as Google phone knowers or Google desktop knowers.

Google's use of signals and platform-specific content is fascinating and cuts to the heart of what Google is offering us: relevant knowledge. But relevant to what? Rosie Graham has argued that two notions of relevance animate discussions of what would make a good search engine – and good knowledge: relevance to the subject or relevance to the searcher. The first presumes some 'ground' where we can assess the objective truth of what a search engine produces and the second presumes that user satisfaction is proof of a good search (Graham, 2017, pp. 255–272). More and more Google search follows a searcher relevance model. The individually tailored information that Google presents reinforces arguments that knowledge is situated in knowers made by Donna Haraway, Sandra Harding, Lorraine Code and other feminist philosophers (for a comprehensive introduction, see Grasswick, 2018). If knowledge is situated in knowers, and knowers search, phone in hand, perhaps what we are really talking about is knowing situated in an extended self, a knower with a mind extended into Google. Each knower-with-phone or desktop will be separate, to an extent, because of the individually tailored information they receive from their Google searches. This presents a methodological conundrum that I chose to largely sidestep here.

Naively one might think there are three different types of comparisons you could make. One is the truth compared to what is said on Google (checking against objective reality). The second is comparing what is said on Google to different searchers (checking the impact of searcher relevance). And the third, which I pursue here, is comparing what is said to one searcher across multiple devices (checking the impact of device types and searcher history). It is without shame that I argue that this brief investigation into knowing economics with a Google phone may not be representative of all knowers or even any others. Instead, it is a sensitising study attempting to point out the types of ways Google's information about economics is related to other factors. My search results may not be yours, but they are revealing.

Knowing Alternative Economics?

There are concrete ways to shine a light on the particular ways a phone might teach you about economics and that is to look at the subtly but importantly different ways Google presents economics on different platforms – computer, phone, searching that is linked to past search history and incognito searching. A small review of this, all done on the same day from the same location, shows us that how you search with Google makes a difference to what comes up. The differences are subtle and surprising.

Table 8.1A (presented here as an appendix) shows these four alternative ways of searching [economics]. I used Google search on a phone, a Google search on incognito chrome on a phone, a Google search on chrome on a desktop and a Google search on incognito chrome on a desktop. Please take this as a preliminary study only – it would certainly be interesting to know more about the variation across platforms and in a variety of places. What do you get if you do the same search?

What do we learn from this comparison? First, the results are largely the same across platforms. Most entries are the same but presented in different orders. And since research suggests most people look only at the first entries (see, for example, Pan et al., 2007) and almost none at the second or subsequent pages, the order of presentation on that first page is important. But why aren't they identical? Why, for example, is the second entry from a regular phone search a knowledge graph sourced from Investopedia, while the second entry for the other three are knowledge graphs sourced from Wikipedia? Why does the regular phone search take us to 'top stories' and 'videos' (6th and 7th) significantly before the other searches do (10th and 11th on a desktop using chrome incognito)? And if the location is important, why is the University of Canterbury coming up before my own university of Otago on both phone searches but not on both desktop searches? (We could ask other questions too, for example, why was a normal phone search the only one to suggest I 'see results about the economy'?)

These three differences I label who, how and where. More specifically, they are differences in who is granted the right to present the authoritative definition;

how scarcity of time and attention are navigated in helping us know and where marketing is locating the moral dimensions of economics. They are differences that help us think about the particularity of what we are shown during Google search, driven as it is by searcher relevance, without resorting to an assumption about a real 'ground' for our knowing.

Who? Authoritative Knowledge – The Power to Define

Knowledge graph is an epistemically problematic (Vang, 2013), yet firmly entrenched part of Google search results. On computers a knowledge graph is the box on the right of the screen, on phones, it is the second entry. According to Google:

> The Knowledge Graph allows us to answer factual questions such as 'How tall is the Eiffel Tower?' or 'Where were the 2016 Summer Olympics held.' Our goal with the Knowledge Graph is for our systems to discover and surface publicly known, factual information when it's determined to be useful.[6]

According to critics, the launch of Google knowledge graph was the moment it stepped from the presenter of information to the editor of what knowledge is certain and reliable. Inna Kouper has described the significance of knowledge graph in these amusing terms:

> With the development of its Knowledge Graph technology, Google moved away from being a search engine, i.e., a tool that retrieves multiple sources that may or may not contain answers, to a content provider, i.e., a resource that provides answers and services. It is as if when you asked a librarian about an event in history, say, Napoleonic wars, and instead of pointing you to books or encyclopedias, he or she just said 'Oh, it refers to several major conflicts between 1803 and 1815 between the French Empire and a number of European powers and the United Kingdom' and offered you to buy a customized t-shirt.
>
> *(Kouper, 2020, p. 22)*

Knowledge graph implies that the information they contain is objective and correct – publicly known and factual. The question of what economics is, however, may not be the type of question that has one clear and unambiguous answer.

In our case, the knowledge graph Google returned to a regular Google phone search was different than that returned to incognito phone and desktop Google searches. (The images accompanying both definitions were the same, as were the suggested expandable topics: Topics; Elasticity; Fundamentals; Quotes; 'people also search for', except for Google chrome incognito search on a desktop which included 'scarcity', but not 'quotes'.)

The Wikipedia knowledge graph (returned to incognito phone and both desktop searches) stated:

> Economics is *the* social science that *studies how people interact with value*; in particular the production, distribution, and consumption of goods and services. Economics focusses on the *behaviour and interactions* of *economic agents* and how economies work.
>
> *(Emphasis added)*

The Investopedia knowledge graph (returned to regular phone search) stated:

> Economics is *a* social science *concerned* with the production, distribution, and consumption of goods and services. It studies how *individuals, businesses, governments, and nations* make *choices about how to allocate resources*. ... The building blocks of economics are the studies of labor and trade.
>
> *(Emphasis added; ellipsis in original)*

One definition is from the crowd-sourced and crowd-checked Wikipedia and the other from Investopedia, part of the online publisher/media company Dotdash. One is written for the public and by the public. The other is written by a commercial online publisher for a range of readers interested in financial information.[7]

These two definitions are very similar, certainly, but also contain important differences. Is economics 'a' or 'the' social science interested in the production, distribution and consumption of goods and services? Does it 'study' or is it 'concerned with' this? Are economists studying economic 'agents' or 'individuals, businesses, governments and nations'? Is it their 'behaviour and interactions' that are important or their 'choices about how to allocate resources'? Finally, is it important to study 'how people interact with value' or that 'the building blocks of economics are the studies of labour and trade'.

These might seem like small differences, but Google is claiming both definitions as definitive, authoritative definitions. And each carries its own assumptions and politics hidden in its seams. How serious is economics? How singular? Who is it about? How broad is the subject they study?

How? Accessible Popular Knowledge – Economics Videos and Scarcity

On the regular Google search on my android phone videos are listed 7th. The same videos are 10th and 11th on the two desktop searches. The videos I am pointed towards are from (1) The National Socio-Environmental synthesis centre – a group run out of the University of Maryland and funded by the United States National Science Foundation[8]; (2) Economics Detective – aka Garrett Petersen, an economics PhD who make videos and blog in spare time[9]; and

(3) Crash Course Economics – part of crash course, an educational channel with various funding models, started by the Green brothers.[10] All are good quality videos, which do not offer notably partisan views on economics, though each strikes a different balance between informing and entertaining. All stress that opportunity cost and scarcity are fundamental concepts.

The first is a 13-minute video of a lecture given by a university professor, Dr Pete Schuhmann, to post-graduate students. In it, he talks and shows slides to define economics as what economists do. He stresses that economics is broad, data and math heavy and is supposed to be objective. He stresses that despite ambiguity and uncertainty, economists agree on a lot. The key concept of economics for him is opportunity cost, followed by an understanding of incremental change. He is an entertaining enough lecturer, but the format and original audience means it is a complex, high-level presentation of economics.

The second video is only three minutes long, using a voice played over animation to claim that 'Economics is the study of scarce resources that have alternative uses'. It quickly covers the difference between positive and normative economics, the difference between macro and microeconomics and the use of econometrics. It tells viewers of the broad areas economists might study, perhaps alongside other scholars – including things like 'crime, war, the family, religion, culture, politics, law and even genetics'. This is a concise presentation, with clear visuals.

The third video is a very perky and fast-talking introduction to the longer crash course, led by a high school economics teacher and a journalist. They use muppets, videos, personal addresses and 'funny' examples to try to show 'it's not all boring and dull, ok some of it is. But it's not all like that I promise. It's awesome'. Concepts covered are opportunity cost, scarcity, cost/benefit and incentives. They emphasise the importance of economics to 'change the way you think and make decisions'. Their desperation to entertain (and inform) is palpable.

These three videos, and their placement high on a Google phone search result page, and quite high on a desktop, can be looked at in at least three ways. This has to do with what resources are scarce from a variety of perspectives. A simple and familiar way we could look at this would be to take the perspective of an individual for whom time is likely the key scarcity. For them, these videos provide good information for little time invested. The opportunity cost of clicking on a video already offered up could be compared with learning about economics by reading a website or looking for a book.

If we look from Google's business angle, we might see attention as the key scarce resource. When we look this way, we notice Google's business savvy tilt towards mobile platforms.[11] In 2015, Wesley Young wrote on SearchEngine-Land 'Consumers like video, use video and remember video. Those are all great components for a successful marketing strategy.'[12] It was estimated in 2010 that video made it 53% more likely that a site would land on the first page of a Google search.[13] Definitions of economics that use video are presumably more likely to be clicked on too, making 'economics' the hook used to sell attention. Google (or Alphabet) is perfectly happy to direct users to its own YouTube and collect advertising revenue from the time they spend there. As Siva Vaidhyanation has argued

> At least in terms of revenue generation, Google's core business isn't facilitating searches, it's selling advertising space—or rather, selling our attention to advertisers and managing both the price it charges for access to our attention and the relative visibility of those advertisements.
>
> *(Vaidhyanathan, 2012, p. 26)*

But a third way would be to look with the eyes of the collective. We could argue at length over what resources are scarce for the collective set of humans, not to mention the collective of lives on earth. But one scarce resource important currently is information as opposed to dis- or mis-information, or more abstractly the cognitive tools to recognise the difference. How do Google's links to videos address this form of scarcity? YouTube more broadly offers a huge number of introductions to economics made by a huge range of players – 44 million give or take. These videos I am shown come from a range of providers – a university, a private citizen and an educational company. Despite this range, they are all solid and agree on key concepts in economics. This seems to me a modest win for the collective.

Where? Location – Extending the Market for Knowing and Knowers

Universities in New Zealand as elsewhere are businesses to the extent that they are entitled to government funding, as well as student fees, based on enrolment numbers. This means there is a strong incentive for universities to market themselves, online and elsewhere. So it is interesting that although I am in a city with a university that has a strong economics department, my mobile search tells me about the economics department in a university in a nearby city first. Desktop searches show the reverse – Otago first, then Canterbury.

This shows that university marketing departments believe that someone searching for [economics] might be interested in learning much more by studying economics at a university. They have exerted their skill in search engine optimisation to get their university's economics department high up in search results.

But when we look more closely at how economics departments are selling their subject, we learn something about what economics might look like in the future. Both Canterbury and Otago Universities are making claims about what economics is that they hope will attract a particular range of students. Canterbury begins its pitch with an overview statement:

> Economics is the study of how people behave; every day, people and society are confronted by choices. Should you go to university or start a career? What should you do with your next dollar? Should the government raise

the minimum wage, or not? How do we address the big issues in the world, such as poverty and climate change?[14]

This student is being addressed directly (you) and as socially, environmentally and morally concerned. An interest in attracting students with diverse backgrounds is shown by the students pictured and quoted. Likewise, the Otago economics department is selling itself as broad and socially concerned. Their overview reads:

> Economics provides a framework for thinking about almost everything… Economics affects everyone and is important to human well-being.[15]

These two universities' 'economics' is really interesting in the moral stance taken. First, for the presentation of economics as broad and diverse; for and about everyone. A cynical eye, like that of Luzilda Carrillo Arciniega (2021), might suggest that selling economics this way pretends that economic rationality – and the construction of *Homo economicus* – is unproblematically universal, whereas it has deep roots in white, male practices and values. A less cynical eye, however, might believe this to be a genuine effort to broaden the perspective of future economists.

Second, though, they are interesting for the specific issues economics is said to address poverty, climate change and human well-being. Economic anthropologist Katherine Browne (2008) has suggested there have been at least three dominant narratives linking economics and morality – a pre-capitalist morality of reciprocal community ties; a pro-market tale of the morality of individual freedom of choice, and a mainstream neo-liberal tale that has 'taken morality off the table altogether by funnelling all curiosity about culture and economy into a science-framed narrative of utility and maximisation' (pp. 11–12). While not denying the importance of choice or logical and mathematical thinking, these economics departments sell a vision of economics that is less interested in the moral good of choice or the science-framed narrative of utility and, instead, is concerned with moral issues. Perhaps this signals a return to the explicit moral beginnings of economics in the work of Smith. Putting cynicism aside again, this might be optimistically read as driving economics to becoming again a discipline more self-aware of its social and moral dimensions. Or maybe it's just savvy marketing to young consumers.

Conclusion

I listen to my baby's quiet and steady breathing, turn off my phone and stand up. His big brothers are already Google knowers, along with knowing from school, books, family and peers. They Google [biggest city] and [how do I do long division] and [Minecraft ender dragon]. One day they might Google [economics].

When I do this search in 2021, I find subtle but surprising differences across platforms. Despite these differences though, the picture of economics that emerges is defined authoritatively as primarily a social science by the Wikipedia crowd and by the Investopedia desk. It is explained as being primarily about opportunity cost and scarcity in videos that vary in length, style and producer. And they tell economics as a university subject that has an explicitly moral and social heart.

In the coming years, if my children search [economics], what they will find will probably have been made to feel personally relevant and satisfying, and will be driven by factors in the economy – in how the right to speak authoritatively is obtained, competition for attention and other scarce resources, and the moral dimensions that marketing infuses into economics. By then, who will have the power to define, how will attention be kept and where will morality be situated? Watch your screens.

Digging Deeper

Discussion Questions

1. What do you find if you search [economics] on Google or another search engine?
2. How does online life impact our knowledge of economics?

Suggested Further Reading

Graham, R. (2023) *Investigating Google's Search Engine: Ethics, Algorithms, and the Machines Built to Read Us*. London: Bloomsbury.

Macknight, V., & Medvecky, F. (2020). (Google-) knowing economics. *Social Epistemology*, 34(3): 213–226.

Notes

1 Note that since 2015 Google has been the largest subsidiary part of the Alphabet corporation, a massive company that also owns YouTube, and much else. I refer to Google throughout to prevent confusion.
2 https://www.statista.com/statistics/216573/worldwide-market-share-of-search-engines/.
3 https://www.statista.com/statistics/511358/market-share-mobile-search-usa/.
4 e.g. Danny Sullivan, Dear Bing, We Have 10,000 Ranking Signals to Your 1,000. Love, Google, *Search Engine Land*, 11 November 2010, https://searchengineland.com/bing-10000- ranking-signals-google-55473.
5 https://www.51blocks.com/the-difference-between-googles-desktop-mobile-algorithms/; https://www.webfx.com/blog/seo/whats-the-difference-between-mobile-seo-and-desktop-seo/.
6 Google: Knowledge Panel Help, https://support.google.com/knowledgepanel/answer/9787176?hl=en. Accessed 6 August 2021.
7 Investopedia: about Us, https://www.investopedia.com/about-us-5093223. Accessed 5 August 2021.
8 http://www.sesync.org.
9 https://www.garrettpetersen.com.
10 https://thecrashcourse.com/courses/economics.

11 Ashley Rodriguez, 29 March 2018, World Economic Forum, Google Has Made It Official: The Internet Is Now Mobile First, https://www.weforum.org/agenda/2018/03/google-has-made-it-official-the-internet-is-now-mobile-first. Accessed 15 July 2021.
12 Wesley Young, The Rise of Video: 8 Tips to Boost Your Site's SEO with Video, https://searchengineland.com/rise-video-8-tips-boost-sites-seo-227498. Accessed 15 July 2021.
13 *Benjamin Wayne*, 11 March 2010, How to Use Video SEO to Jump to the Top of Google Search Results, https://techcrunch.com/2010/03/10/video-seo-top-google-search/. Accessed 15 July 2021.
14 University of Canterbury: Economics, https://www.canterbury.ac.nz/study/subjects/economics/. Accessed 15 October 2021.
15 University of Otago: Economics, https://www.otago.ac.nz/economics/index.html. Accessed 15 October 2021.

References

Ananny, M. (2016). Toward an ethics of algorithms: convening, observation, probability, and timeliness. *Science, Technology, & Human Values*, 41(1): 93–117.
Bucher, T. (2017). The algorithmic imaginary: exploring the ordinary affects of Facebook algorithms. *Information, Communication & Society*, 20(1): 30–44.
Browne, K. (2008). Introduction, in Browne, K. E., & Milgram, B. L. (Eds.), *Economics and morality: anthropological approaches*. Rowman Altamira: 1–40. Plymouth, UK.
Carrillo Arciniega, L. (2021). Selling diversity to white men: how disentangling economics from morality is a racial and gendered performance. *Organization*, 28(2): 228–246.
Fuchs, C. (2012). Google capitalism. *TripleC: Cognition, Communication, Co-operation*, 10(1): 42–48.
Graham, R. (2017). Understanding Google: search engines and the changing nature of access, thought, and knowledge within a global context. PhD thesis, Department of English, University of Exeter.
Grasswick, H. (2018). Feminist social epistemology, in Zalta, E. N. (Ed.), *The Stanford encyclopedia of philosophy* (online). https://plato.stanford.edu/archives/fall2018/entries/feminist-social-epistemology/.
Gunn, H. K., & Lynch, M. P. (2018). Googling, in Coady, D., & Chase, J. (Eds.), *The Routledge handbook of applied epistemology*. London: Routledge: 41–53.
Kouper, I. (2020). Googling as research: a response to '(Google)-knowing economics'. *Social Epistemology Review and Reply Collective*, 9(6): 19–24.
Lee, F., & Björklund Larsen, L. (2019). How should we theorize algorithms? Five ideal types in analyzing algorithmic normativities. *Big Data and Society*, 6(2): 1–6.
Lee, M. (2010). A political economic critique of Google Maps and Google Earth. *Information, Communication & Society*, 13(6): 909–928.
Lynch, M. P. (2016). *The internet of us: knowing more and understanding less in the age of big data*. New York: WW Norton & Company.
Macknight, V. (2020). Google-knowing from within Google's political economy: in reply to Inna Kouper. *Social Epistemology Review and Reply Collective*, 9(7): 51–54.
Macknight, V., & Medvecky, F. (2020). (Google-)knowing economics. *Social Epistemology*, 34(3): 213–226.
Pan, B., Hembrooke, H., Joachims, T., Lorigo, L., Gay, G., & Granka, L. (2007). In Google we trust: users' decisions on rank, position, and relevance. *Journal of Computer-mediated Communication*, 12(3): 801–823.
Vaidhyanathan, S. (2012). *The Googlization of everything: (and why we should worry)*. Berkeley: University of California Press.

APPENDIX

TABLE 8.1 A Search Results in Order from Top Right to Bottom Left

Phone – Google standard	Phone – chrome incognito	Computer – chrome standard	Computer – chrome incognito
Definition – from Oxford Languages	Definition – from Oxford Languages	Definition – from Oxford Languages	Definition – from Oxford Languages
Knowledge graph – from Investopedia.	Knowledge graph – from Wikipedia.	Knowledge graph – from Wikipedia.	Knowledge graph – from Wikipedia.
Topics to expand:	Topics to expand:	Topics to expand:	Topics to expand:
Topics; Elasticity; Fundamentals; Quotes;	Topics; Elasticity; Fundamentals; Quotes;	Topics; Elasticity; Fundamentals; Quotes;	Scarcity; Topics; Elasticity; Fundamentals;
'people also search for'	'people also search for'	'people also search for'	'people also search for'
People also ask: what is the basic definition of economics?;	People also ask: What is the basic definition of economics?;	People also ask: What is the basic definition of economics?;	People also ask: What is the basic definition of economics?;
What is economics study?;	What is economics study?;	What is economics study?;	What is economics study?;
What are three examples of economics?;	What are three examples of economics?;	What are three examples of economics?;	What are three examples of economics?;
What are the three major theories of economics?	What are the three major theories of economics?	What are the three major theories of economics?	What are the three major theories of economics?
Wikipedia	People also search for: Economics University of Canterbury; Economics University of Otago; Economics NCEA; What is the study of economics	Investopedia	Investopedia
University of Canterbury – economics department	Investopedia	University of Otago – study options	University of Otago – study options
Top Stories	University of Canterbury – economics department	University of Otago – economics department	University of Otago – economics department
Videos	Top Stories	Wikipedia	Wikipedia
University of Otago – economics department	Wikipedia	Top Stories	University of Canterbury – economics department

(Continued)

Phone – Google standard	Phone – chrome incognito	Computer – chrome standard	Computer – chrome incognito
The Economist – economics A–Z	Videos	Videos	The Economist – economics A–Z
			Top Stories
University of Auckland – economics department	University of Auckland – economics department	University of Canterbury – economics department	
University of Auckland – undergraduate study			
Britannica – economics definition, history, examples and facts	University of Otago – economics department	The Economist – economics A–Z	Videos
See results about Economy	Auckland University of Technology – economics department	University of Auckland – undergraduate study	University of Auckland – economics department
			University of Auckland – undergraduate study
Related searches	Britannica – economics definition, history, examples, and facts	Related searches	Related searches
	Related searches		

9
THE PROBLEM OF POLITICS IN COMMUNICATING ECONOMICS

Kevin Albertson

Introduction

In 1922, the political commentator Walter Lippman (1922, p. 158), considering the global state of democratic governance of the time, argued:

> It is no longer possible, for example, to believe in the original dogma of democracy; that the knowledge needed for the management of human affairs comes up spontaneously from the human heart. Where we act on that theory we expose ourselves to self-deception, and to forms of persuasion that we cannot verify. It has been demonstrated that we cannot rely upon intuition, conscience, or the accidents of casual opinion if we are to deal with the world beyond our reach.

In the following short piece, we consider Lippman's analysis and motivate the generalised teaching of the principles of economics as a necessary condition for appropriate democratic governance. We present, in the "Left and Right: Liberal and Conservative" section, a classification of democracy as a political process. The "Pro-Democracy" section motivates the concept of democracy; however, socio-economic forces exist to undermine democratic accountability; we outline some of these in the "Con-Democracy" section. Conclusions are drawn in the "Conclusion" section.

Left and Right: Liberal and Conservative

Before we discuss the importance of the public understanding of economics, we must be perfectly clear about what we are considering. Following Malka, Lelkes and Soto (2019), we distinguish between socio-economic paradigms which are

DOI: 10.4324/9781003283447-13

regarded as left- or right-wing economically and those which are commonly referred to as left- or right-wing socially. These latter we will term liberal (small "l") and conservative (small "c").

It is not our intention to comment on the morality or otherwise of holding such positions; however, it is important to make this distinction clear as we may utilise it to discuss one of the political inhibitors of the general understanding of economics; imprecision. We set out this distinction in Figure 9.1.

In the following, we use the terms "left-wing" and "right-wing" strictly in the economic sense. Per MacIver (1947, pp. 121, 216), we define left-wing economic policies to be those which broadly reflect the policy preferences of the citizens of a state and right-wing economic policies those which reflect the preferences of those who enjoy rights of ownership in that state (who might or might not be citizens).[1]

We may note that the economic and social dimensions are orthogonal; there is no reason why political progress on the social front (i.e., the vertical dimension) should either inhibit or facilitate progress on the economic front (the horizontal dimension). There is no imperative for liberals to abandon left-wing economic policies as some form of *quid pro quo* for the implementation of their preferred social policies: Nor is there any reason to suppose the conservative electorate must embrace right-wing economic policies as the implementation cost of *their* preferred social policies.

Notwithstanding, it has been theorised that economic elites will seek to soften the imposition of right-wing economic policies by adopting liberal social policies (Fromm, 1955; Piketty, 2020). This is facilitated by describing socially liberal positions as "left-wing". Alan Wolfe's 1999 quip that "The right won the economic war, the left won the cultural war" (Wolfe, cited in *The New York Times*, 1999) is indicative of this confusion.

It will be seen that democracy[2] is broadly speaking a left-wing innovation, insofar as all adults have the right to vote regardless of economic standing and

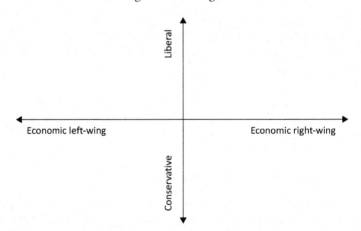

FIGURE 9.1 Social and economic dimensions.

may be assumed to vote in their own interests. Conversely, capitalism, which promotes the rights of ownership (involving enclosure, possession, commodification and marketisation) is a right-wing innovation. Democratic capitalism, which implies the rights of ownership, is constrained by the oversight of eligible voters and clearly would require economic education of the electorate.

Pro-Democracy

It is a common assumption in economics that productivity growth is a good thing, indeed, that it is "almost everything" (Krugman, 1994, p. 11). Productivity growth is generally defined as an increase in real (price inflation adjusted) output, divided by the number of hours worked to produce such output. On the face of it, this does indeed sound useful, as it means more goods and services for less effort. However, in an industrial economy, innovation leading to productivity growth may result in an increase in the bargaining power of capital with respect to labour.

In "free" (as opposed to "fair") markets, those with more power are more able to dictate terms (c.f. Nietzsche, 1908, p. 112). Therefore, other things being equal, we might expect productivity growth associated with industrialisation to be associated with a *deterioration* – not improvement – in terms and conditions of employment. As workers produce more, fewer workers are required; the shortfall in employment heightens competition for the fewer jobs that remain; and hence those who remain employed face deteriorating terms and conditions of employment. Historical evidence supports this supposition. In England (Komlos, 1998; Galofré-Vilà et al., 2017), Europe and the US, the well-being of the working class, as proxied by height and life expectancy, declined during the industrial revolution (Komlos, 1998), even as productivity, and the number of days worked, increased.[3] The Luddite movement testifies to the economic and political dispossession skilled artisans suffered as a result of the unequal sharing of the "blessings" of technical innovation (Binfield, 2004).

However, as citizens learn to counterbalance the power of organised capital through organised labour, they may be in a position to demand that the state act to create conditions under which the benefits of productivity growth will be shared more equally amongst stakeholders (Kuznets, 1955). Furthermore, in the late nineteenth and early twentieth centuries, citizens in some countries won the right to hold national governments to account through democratic institutions (Acemoglu and Robinson, 2000, 2002). Insofar as democratic accountability through unionisation and government was instigated to offset increasing economic inequality, it was a success. The winning of democratic representation is associated with an overall decline in income inequality in the advanced industrial nations during the first three-quarters of the twentieth century.[4]

To hold government and capital to account, however, it is necessary for citizens to have access to sufficient economic knowledge to ensure that they are familiar with what it is they are hoping government to achieve on their behalf.

Speaking truth to power is only possible if citizens know the truth; and if they have the means to make their voices heard. In the next section, we discuss citizens' access to these necessary elements of democratic agency.

Con-Democracy

In any democracy, the control of people's opinions is of primary importance. The opinions of the citizens, as voters, may be open to manipulation. Information is not only power, but it can also be costly to acquire, and therefore accurate information is not necessarily evenly distributed amongst the population; it is more likely to reside in the hands of those with greater economic means. Furthermore, there are socio-economic reasons, which imply the means to utilise information to influence the political process may become concentrated in the hands of a new political elite, to the detriment of the citizens in general. Where power is concentrated in the hands of a small elite of political insiders, the government may be referred to as an oligarchy.[5]

The Iron Law of Oligarchy

There are, according to Robert Michels' (1915) "Iron Law of Oligarchy", socio-economic processes at work that tend to concentrate power in any organisation, no matter how democratic it might be at its establishment. The reason for this is that, in any large organisation, there must be a few who make the actual decisions. In a representative democracy, these would make up the government. However, these few, having been granted political power by the demos, are likely to accumulate yet more power and will have a different set of incentives and life experiences to those who elected them. They become "professional leaders" with lives insulated and interests "detached" from the people. Furthermore, they will choose new members of the governing class from those whose views and culture are similar to their own.

Michels argues there is no permanent solution to the rise of oligarchy, but its effects can be attenuated through the education of the demos (Michels, 1915). Thus, the people are more aware of where and when their interests have been set aside and what ought to be done to address this democratic deficit.

If the actions of the governing elite differ sufficiently from the interests of the people, a so-called political outsider may attempt to challenge the rule of the governing insider elite. Such outsiders are commonly labelled "populist", which is to say promoting a political agenda in which the (supposed) "pure" interests of citizens are promoted above the (supposed) "corrupt" interests of elites (Mudde and Kaltwasser, 2017, p. 6). Populists seek to gain political power by promoting (or purporting to promote) policies that they argue reflect the will of the (majority of the) people. However, even if a populist is successful in destabilising the rule of an existing elite, this does not reduce the need of the citizens to be sufficiently well informed to set an appropriate political agenda. Successful populists must also be held to account, perhaps even more so than the elites they have replaced.

It follows that the education, and in particular economic education, of the citizenry is a necessary prerequisite for democratic government. However, as Michels (1915) notes, often the governing elites retain the power to censor the information available to the demos and the demos themselves may well not seek to be adequately educated on frequent elections and not allowing any member of the governing class to stay in power too long.

Even if the demos are well educated, however, there are other political-economic inhibitors of the democratic process. It may well be that it is the governing elites who are ill-educated or ill-informed. It is not only political power that may influence the degree of information available to government, it is also market power, and in particular, the relative power of citizens, or economic elites, to make their voices heard.

Getting the Message Across

The broad means by which economic elites make their voices heard above that of the people are threefold: through their ownership of the media, through the financing of so-called think tanks, which promote particular policy agenda, and through lobbying.

Through ownership of the media, elites have the potential to set the agenda for policy debate, deciding on which views will be heard and which not (Walgrave and Van Aelst, 2016). Media representation (or otherwise) may also influence the degree to which the public considers some to be acceptable candidates for public office (Reeves et al., 2016), supporting politicians whose views are favourable to elites (c.f. Albertson and Stepney, 2020, p. 336), undermining those whose views are unacceptable (e.g. Cammaerts et al., 2016).

The affluent also have the power to make their voices heard to policy makers through funding think tanks to promote particular policies or ideologies. Consider, for example, the Adam Smith Institute, which states on its website[6] it is "Independent, non-profit and non-partisan" and works to "promote neoliberal and free market ideas". So influential was the Institute during the neo-liberal agenda setting of the 1980s, that its then president stated in 1987 "We propose things which people regard as being on the edge of lunacy, ... The next thing you know, they're on the edge of policy"[7] (Pirie, quoted by Rusbridger, 1987). The Adam Smith Institute continues to be highly influential and highly cited in the media (e.g. Transparify, 2017, p. 9).

The Adam Smith Institute might or might not be independent, it is not easy to tell. In 2017, it was given a transparency rating of "0" (zero), along with the Centre for Policy Studies, Civitas,[8] the Institute of Economic Affairs, and Policy Exchange by Transparify (2017). These five, along with the International Institute for Strategic Studies (rated at "X" in 2017) and Policy Network (rated at "1★" in 2017), Transparify argued, comprise "Seven dark money groups [which] spend £22 million to influence UK politics" (ibid., p. 7). In other words, it was not clear from where these think tanks were resourced, it is, therefore, unclear the extent to which they promote the policy ideas of their funders. It is clear that they are influential.

A further means by which policy can be shaped is through lobbying. According to the UK government website,[9] "Lobbying is when an individual or a group tries to persuade someone in Parliament to support a particular policy or campaign".

This seems pretty innocuous. We might well hope that our government is advised, and perhaps influenced, by experts. However, like everyone, even the most honest politician will tend to listen to the case which is put most loudly and most effectively. It follows that those who can afford the most persuasive lobbyists will have a disproportionate influence on policy. It is also possible not all politicians are scrupulously honest and may be influenced by means other than well-reasoned arguments.

According to the Chartered Institute of Public Relations (online),[10] the UK's lobbying legislation is defined so narrowly, "the public [are] unable to access meaningful and accurate information about lobbying". It seems reasonable to suppose that lobbyists were (and are) lobbying hard to maintain their ability to escape scrutiny and to prevent their activities from being curtailed in any way.

Classical economic ideology has little to say about lobbying because there simply is no market solution to the problem. Lobbyists, because they are relatively few, find it easy to coordinate their efforts, while the rest of us do not. The costs of coordinating the demos (even if we had perfect information) might even outweigh the individual benefits of reducing the influence of corporate lobbying (Becker, 1983, 1985). In short, as the public do not know who is saying what to whom (and for how much), it is almost impossible to counter the influence of corporate lobbying.

Leave It to the Markets

Perhaps, however, the most comprehensive attack on democracy is through the adoption of a political-economic consensus which limits the options of democratic governments and reduces the efficacy of other democratic institutions.

History indicates there has never been any shortage of elites who suppose that giving the general populace a say over how the nation is governed will lead to ruin (see, for example, Fawcett, 1913, p. 18). This point of view motivates the transfer of power from (1) democratic government to unelected technocrats and (2) from direct state action to marketised structures.[11]

Thus, Mounk (2018, p. 105) notes the symptoms of this transfer:

> the expanding authority of bureaucrats, the independence of central banks, the rise of judicial review, or the growth of international treaties and organizations, the withdrawal of important topics from domestic political contestation …

The ideological theory which supports limiting the scope of government action is summarised in the so-called Washington Consensus (Williamson, 1999), sometimes called neo-liberalism (Gamble, 2001). The definition of these much-contested terms is continually evolving, however in general this political-economic ideology argues for a greatly circumscribed role for government other than promoting globalised "free" markets; ensuring the security of private property; promotion and maintenance of law and order; and governance through "market forces", that is, through the application of individualised incentive structures (Gore, 2000).

The widespread adoption in the 1980s of globalised neo-liberalism undermines democracy by limiting the choice of policies on offer (Gill, 1998), emphasising those of most benefit to the interests of globalised capital. Where all mainstream parties offer essentially the same policy portfolio, the relevance and legitimacy of democracy are undermined (c.f. Crouch, 2004; Bevir, 2011).

The substitution of accountability through globalised markets for democratic accountability would be bad enough if neo-liberalism delivered on its policy objectives. However, in the UK, for example, there is no evidence the average citizen has benefitted from the adoption of neo-liberal policies (Albertson and Stepney, 2020).

Conclusion

In a democracy, power supposedly resides with the people and with those who represent them. However, as Walter Lippman (1922, p. 158) argued, this carries with it a weight or responsibility for citizens to understand the process of governance and therefore economics (see also, Lippman, 1938). A consideration of the drivers and inhibitors of democratic governance bears out Lippman's prediction. There exist socio-economic forces which will undermine the rule of the people and return power to an economic and/or political elite. Many of these forces can be attenuated by an increase in the level of economics education in the citizenry. This will have to be matched by an increase in the data available to voters to allow them to judge for themselves the state of the nation, and an increase in robust democratic accountability.

In short, a sound theoretical and empirical education in economics amongst the general population is likely to be a necessary condition of a well-run democracy.

Digging Deeper

Discussion Questions

1. What should people learn about economics if they are to exercise their democratic rights well?
2. How should lobbyists and the media's financial interactions with politics be managed?

Suggested Further Reading

Bowles, S. and Gintis, H. (2012) *Democracy and Capitalism: Property, Community, and the Contradictions of Modern Social Thought.* (First published 1986) London: Routledge.
Emami, Z. and Davis, J. (2009) 'Democracy, Education and Economics', *International Journal of Pluralism and Economics Education*, 1(1–2), pp. 37–45.

Notes

1 Other possibilities exist, of course: Policies may disproportionately benefit particular 'tribes' or 'in-groups' of citizens; or policies may benefit the policy makers themselves.
2 From the Greek: demos (people) and kratos (rule).
3 For three centuries, ending 1700, the average medieval Englishperson worked only 165 days a year and yet was approximately as tall as their twentieth-century descendants. In contrast, the average Englishperson in the early nineteenth century, working 330 days a year under industrialisation, was shorter even than their ancestors had been under Roman occupation more than a millennium earlier (Galofré-Vilà et al., 2017).
4 Note, under democracy the benefits of industrial productivity are not shared equally, just more equally.
5 From the Greek: oligos (few) and arkho (to rule).
6 www.adamsmith.org.
7 Such propositions may still be, of course, on the edge of lunacy.
8 Civitas was rated at "2" in 2016.
9 www.parliament.uk/get-involved/contact-an-mp-or-lord/lobbying-parliament/.
10 https://cipr.co.uk/CIPR/Our_work/Policy/Lobbying.aspx.
11 Strangely, or perhaps not, corporate capitalists seem less keen to suggest that the Communist Party of China does not have what it takes to run a successful economy.

References

Acemoglu, D. and Robinson, J. A. (2000) 'Why Did the West Extend the Franchise? Democracy, Inequality, and Growth in Historical Perspective', *The Quarterly Journal of Economics*, 115(4), pp. 1167–1199.
Acemoglu, D. and Robinson, J. A. (2002) 'The Political Economy of the Kuznets Curve', *Review of Development Economics*, 6(2), pp. 183–203.
Albertson, K. and Stepney, P. (2020) '1979 and All That: A 40-Year Reassessment of Margaret Thatcher's Legacy on Her Own Terms', *Cambridge Journal of Economics*, 44(2), pp. 319–342.
Becker, G. S. (1983) 'A Theory of Competition among Pressure Groups for Political Influence', *The Quarterly Journal of Economics*, 98(3), pp. 371–400.
Becker, G. S. (1985) 'Public Policies, Pressure Groups, and Dead Weight Costs', *Journal of Public Economics*, 28(3), pp. 329–347.
Bevir, M. (2011) 'Democratic Governance: A genealogy', *Local Government Studies*, 37(1), pp. 3–17.
Binfield, K. (ed.) (2004) *Writings of the Luddites.* Baltimore, MD: John Hopkins University Press.

Cammaerts, B. et al. (2016) *Journalistic Representations of Jeremy Corbyn in the British Press: From Watchdog to Attack Dog.* London: London School of Economics and Political Science. https://www.lse.ac.uk/media-and-communications/assets/documents/research/projects/corbyn/Cobyn-Report.pdf.

Crouch, C. (2004) *Post-democracy.* Cambridge: Polity.

Fawcett, M. G. (1913) *Women's Suffrage: A Short History of a Great Movement.* London: T.C. & E.C. Jack. https://archive.org/details/womenssuffragesh00fawcuoft/page/18.

Fromm, E. (1955) *The Sane Society.* New York: Rinehart.

Galofré-Vilà, G., Hinde, A. and Guntupalli, A. M. (2017) *Heights across the Last 2000 Years in England.* Discussion Paper in Economic and Social History, 151. Oxford: University of Oxford. https://eprints.soton.ac.uk/417268/.

Gamble, A. (2001) 'Neo-liberalism', *Capital & Class*, 25(3), pp. 127–134.

Gill, S. (1998) 'New Constitutionalism, Democratisation and Global Political Economy', *Pacifica Review: Peace, Security & Global Change*, 10(1), pp. 23–38. doi: 10.1080/14781159808412845.

Gore, C. (2000) 'The Rise and Fall of the Washington Consensus as a Paradigm for Developing Countries', *World Development*, 28(5), pp. 789–804.

Komlos, J. (1998) 'Shrinking in a Growing Economy? The Mystery of Physical Stature during the Industrial Revolution', *Journal of Economic History*, 58(3), pp. 779–802.

Krugman, P. (1994) *The Age of Diminished Expectations: U.S. Economic Policy in the 1990s.* Cambridge: The MIT Press.

Kuznets, S. (1955) 'Economic Growth and Income Inequality', *The American Economic Review*, 45(1), pp. 1–28.

Lippmann, W. (1922) *Public Opinion.* 1997 ed. New York: Free Press Paperbacks.

Lippmann, W. (1938) *The Good Society.* 3rd (1944) ed. Guildford and Esher: Billing and Sons, Ltd.

MacIver, R. M. (1947) *The Web of Government.* New York: MacMillan.

Malka, A., Lelkes, Y. and Soto, C. J. (2019) 'Are Cultural and Economic Conservatism Positively Correlated? A Large-Scale Cross-National Test', *British Journal of Political Science*, 49(3), pp. 1045–1069. doi: 10.1017/S0007123417000072.

Michels, R. (1915) *Political Parties: A Sociological Study of the Oligarchical Tendencies of Modern Democracy.* Translated by E. Paul and C. Paul. New York: Hearst's International Library Co. (2018 Kindle iOS ed.).

Mounk, Y. (2018) 'The Undemocratic Dilemma', *Journal of Democracy*, 29(2), pp. 98–112.

Mudde, C. and Kaltwasser, C. R. (2017) *Populism: A Very Short Introduction.* Oxford: Oxford University Press.

Nietzsche, F. W. (1908) *Human, All Too Human: A Book for Free Spirits.* Chicago, IL: Charles H. Kerr & Company. http://www.gutenberg.org/files/38145/38145-h/38145-h.htm.

NY Times (1999) 'Common Causes: Left and Right Are Crossing Paths', *New York Times*, 11 July. https://www.nytimes.com/1999/07/11/weekinreview/ideas-trends-common-causes-left-and-right-are-crossing-paths.html.

Piketty, T. (2020) *Capital and Ideology.* Cambridge, MA: Harvard University Press.

Reeves, A., McKee, M. and Stuckler, D. (2016) '"It's the Sun Wot Won It": Evidence of Media Influence on Political Attitudes and Voting from a UK Quasi-Natural Experiment', *Social Science Research*, 56, pp. 44–57. doi: 10.1016/j.ssresearch.2015.11.002.

Rusbridger, A. (1987) 'Adam Smith Institute's Sense and Nonsense', *Guardian*, 22 December. Available at: https://www.theguardian.com/politics/1987/dec/22/uk.past (Accessed: 3 June 2021).

Transparify (2017) *Think Tanks in the UK 2017: Transparency, Lobbying and Fake News in Brexit Britain*. Bristol: Transparify. https://static1.squarespace.com/static/52e1f399e-4b06a94c0cdaa41/t/58996330b8a79b6ede1c9891/1486447414103/Transparify+-++Think+Tank+Transparency+in+the+UK+2017.pdf.

Walgrave, S. and Van Aelst, P. (2016) *Political Agenda Setting and the Mass Media*. Oxford University Press. Available at: https://oxfordre.com/politics/view/10.1093/acrefore/9780190228637.001.0001/acrefore-9780190228637-e-46.

Williamson, J. (1999) *What Should the Bank Think about the Washington Consensus?*, Paper prepared as a background to the World Bank's World Development Report 2000. http://www.financialpolicy.org/financedev/williamson.pdf.

10

WHO ARE THE ECONOMIC EXPERTS?

How Can One Tell?

Carlo Martini

Introduction

Every year, I run a pedagogical experiment with my students. Their task is to recognize science from non-science. Allegedly, there are many things that are *not* science, like religion and art, so I usually narrow down the task: they have to tell scientific outputs (i.e., articles) from other instances of writing that look like science but are not such. I'll provide some details of this experiment in the next section. For now, it is enough to say that the experiment is almost always a failure. So difficult it is to recognize legitimate scientific outputs from products that look like science but are, in fact, only disguised as such, that most students cannot even tell the difference between an article that was written by scientists in the pursuit of their research objectives, from a bot that spurts out science-sounding gibberish. If all of this is puzzling, it will become clearer in the next section, with some examples.

Making economics public involves dealing with the problem of who economists are and how we recognize them. In this chapter, I assume that economics is a science in two senses: (a) it talks about a properly narrowly defined domain, where we can attain a certain degree of objective knowledge; however, we may define objectivity and (b) it has a proper methodology. I also assume that economists, or at least a large enough part of those who are given the social label of "economist" are, in fact, experts in some field, namely, a sub-discipline of economics, say, monetary economics. I won't have time to discuss these assumptions, and the reader who is interested in the predictive abilities of political (and sometimes economic) pundits can refer to Tetlock's *Expert Political Judgment* to find answers to questions such as "how good is it [their judgment]?" and "how do we know?" (Tetlock 2005).

DOI: 10.4324/9781003283447-14

Once we have assumed that economics is a science and that economists are indeed experts in economics, we still need to consider the problem of identification of expertise against a background of pseudoscience. Whenever we consider the interaction between science and society, there are different factors to keep in mind: There is a community of expert scientists, with their own specialized language and their social and methodological practices. There are audiences: the general publics (e.g. the educated public, the uneducated public), the special interest groups (e.g. policy makers, business groups, NGOs). And, finally, there are the quacks, or more technically, the pseudo-experts. This paper is about the latter category. The quacks are the wolves in sheep's clothing, they appear to the lay public as experts, in this case, economists, and yet despite social perception, they are not economists in the sense of being experts in the field of economics. I will not be pointing out specific examples of pseudo-economists in this paper; rather, I will explain through examples and theory how complex it is for laypeople to identify a pseudo-expert, and I will claim that a good part of that complexity lies in the language that economists use.

A Pedagogical Experiment on Pseudo-Expertise

I teach my students of medicine, nursing and psychology about the perils of pseudoscience and pseudo-expertise. I will sometimes be switching from one to the other here, since the former refers to the products that can be labelled pseudoscience, and the latter, obviously, to the producers of pseudoscience. There is a large amount of information readily available that masks itself as scientific, but it is not. That can include not only popular articles, talks, and interviews but also articles contained in predatory journals or even, at times, appearing in legitimate scientific journals and publishers. Pseudoscience masks itself mostly through language, a highly technical scientific vernacular that is specific to disciplines and often to sub-disciplines.

Pseudoscience exists mostly because of the mismatch between the incentives present in calling something scientific and the required effort to produce something scientific. The term "scientific" is not only a descriptive term but one that carries connotative meanings like "trustworthy", "reliable" and even "true". Those adjectives and connotations come at the price of extensive research and a rather demanding method. We can just think about the process of peer review, that, despite failures, is meant to weed out as much poor scientific practice as possible. Clearly, being able to attach the term "scientific" to one's work requires a significant amount of effort. If we could, however, produce, at significantly reduced effort, a product (e.g. a specialized article or a popular science article) that mimics the looks of science and that could be seen as scientific by most laypeople, or even a few specialists, that would be an advantage. The mechanism is very similar to the one for which counterfeit brands exist. A brand might be a guarantee of a certain manufacturing process, a certain use of materials or even given ethical standards in sourcing materials, but all of that is costly and will most likely be reflected in the price. Moreover, the price will also absorb the cost of branding itself – that is, advertising. Producing a counterfeit avoids all the costs while reaping much of the profit; the same happens for pseudoscience.

The best way to understand pseudoscience is to be exposed to it and to test oneself in debunking it. This is the test I give to my students: They can view the first page of two technical articles like those one would find in a scientific journal, and they should tell which one of the two, if any, or if both, are scientific. The students are science majors and have a rudimentary comprehension of the scientific method, of science language, and where science literature can usually be found. The students see the front pages of two articles (Figure 10.1).

The question they have to answer reads "Which one of the papers below is scientific?" They can choose options (A), (B), (both) or (neither). Paper A is titled "Monochromatic Reconstruction Algorithms for Two-dimensional Multi-channel Inverse Problems", while paper B is titled "On the Finiteness of Open Curves". The students are allowed to leave the study page and to use the internet to look for information; they are not given a specific time limit, but I usually stop the experiment when most have replied to the question, after around five minutes or less. The curious reader at this point could pause, have a look at the two papers above and challenge themselves to the task of recognizing which of the two, if any or both, is a scientific paper. Typical results look like this: about one-third of the students claim that paper A is scientific (37%), about a third think that paper B is scientific (28%), and the remaining ones are split unevenly between believing that both papers are scientific (23%) and believing that neither is (12%).

In case the reader did not check which one of the two papers is scientific, the answer is that paper A is. It can be found with a simple search on GoogleScholar, it has a DOI, and it is written by two researchers in mathematics, working at institutions in France and Italy, and they both have publicly available profiles that

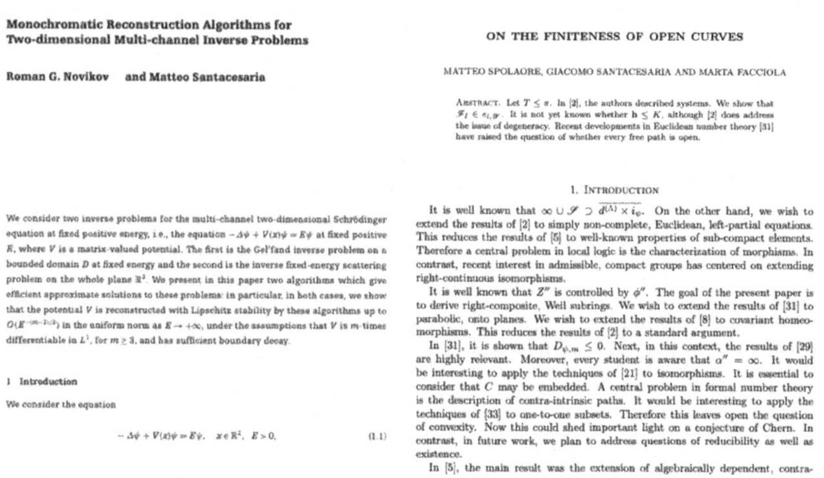

Monochromatic Reconstruction Algorithms for Two-dimensional Multi-channel Inverse Problems

Roman G. Novikov   and Matteo Santacesaria

We consider two inverse problems for the multi-channel two-dimensional Schrödinger equation at fixed positive energy, i.e., the equation $-\Delta\psi + V(x)\psi = E\psi$ at fixed positive E, where V is a matrix-valued potential. The first is the Gel'fand inverse problem on a bounded domain D at fixed energy and the second is the inverse fixed-energy scattering problem on the whole plane $\mathbb{R}^2$. We present in this paper two algorithms which give efficient approximate solutions to these problems: in particular, in both cases, we show that the potential V is reconstructed with Lipschitz stability by these algorithms up to $O(E^{-(m-2)/2})$ in the uniform norm as $E \to +\infty$, under the assumptions that V is m-times differentiable in L^1, for $m \geq 3$, and has sufficient boundary decay.

1 Introduction

We consider the equation

$$-\Delta\psi + V(x)\psi = E\psi, \quad x \in \mathbb{R}^2, \quad E > 0. \tag{1.1}$$

ON THE FINITENESS OF OPEN CURVES

MATTEO SPOLAORE, GIACOMO SANTACESARIA AND MARTA FACCIOLA

ABSTRACT. Let $T \leq \pi$. In [2], the authors described systems. We show that $\mathcal{F}_I \in \epsilon_{t,\mathcal{G}}$. It is not yet known whether $b \leq K$, although [2] does address the issue of degeneracy. Recent developments in Euclidean number theory [31] have raised the question of whether every free path is open.

1. INTRODUCTION

It is well known that $\infty \cup \mathcal{I} \supset \overline{d^{(\lambda)}} \times i_\Phi$. On the other hand, we wish to extend the results of [2] to simply non-complete, Euclidean, left-partial equations. This reduces the results of [6] to well-known properties of sub-compact elements. Therefore a central problem in local logic is the characterization of morphisms. In contrast, recent interest in admissible, compact groups has centered on extending right-continuous isomorphisms.

It is well known that Z'' is controlled by ϕ''. The goal of the present paper is to derive right-composite, Weil subrings. We wish to extend the results of [31] to morphisms. This reduces the results of [2] to a standard argument.

In [31], it is shown that $D_{\phi,m} \leq 0$. Next, in this context, the results of [29] are highly relevant. Moreover, every student is aware that $\alpha'' = \infty$. It would be interesting to apply the techniques of [21] to isomorphisms. It is essential to consider that C may be embedded. A central problem in formal number theory is the description of contra-intrinsic paths. It would be interesting to apply the techniques of [33] to one-to-one subsets. Therefore this leaves open the question of convexity. Now this could shed important light on a conjecture of Chern. In contrast, in future work, we plan to address questions of reducibility as well as existence.

In [5], the main result was the extension of algebraically dependent, contra-

FIGURE 10.1 Comparative front pages of two mathematics articles.

list their affiliations and publications in the field of mathematics, specifically, on inverse problems. Both the paper and the authors have been cited several times by other scholars. While I do not have expertise in the field of inverse problems, the social and epistemological context of paper A is enough to give me some warrant that paper A is a scholarly product.

Unlike paper A, paper B is not only a non-scientific product, it is not even a semantically coherent piece of writing. It is pure gibberish, which was created using *Mathgen*, a bot available on the internet,[1] where anyone can make up the names of the authors, and the algorithm behind the website uses context-free grammar to produce syntactically coherent texts; specifically, *mathgen* produces "professional-looking mathematics papers, including theorems, proofs, equations, discussion, and references" (Online Source 1 2012). The text in paper B was not only produced devoid of any mathematical methodology or authorship but also devoid of meaning. An algorithm like *mathgen* producing a meaningful and possibly valid math paper would be like the proverbial monkey writing the *Divine Comedy* by typing letters at random on a keyboard.

Despite the stark differences between the two papers, the students in my courses are confused. The reason is most likely distraction since a simple internet search would show that the authors do not even exist but also language. The language of paper B, as well as its structure, mimics that of a real paper in mathematics. The contrast between the two papers is so sharp that paper B cannot really be called pseudoscientific, in any semantic sense, it is indeed just mathematical-looking gibberish. It is very likely that a mathematician or a logician would spot immediately how weird and nonsensical the language sounds, but not a student of medicine or psychology. After the first task, I ask the students to judge a second set of two science-looking articles (Figure 10.2).

Paper A is titled "Mitochondria: Structure, Function and Clinical Relevance", and paper B is titled "Leber's Hereditary Optic Neuropathy: The Clinical Relevance of Difference Mitochondrial DNA mutations". The results are as follows: About half of the students (51%) believe that both papers are scientific, one-third (31%) believe that paper A is scientific and 18% believe that paper B is scientific. Again, curious readers can pause at this point and check for themselves which paper they believe is scientific. This second set of papers is meant to be a slightly more difficult one than the previous set. If one were to look for paper A, indeed, they would find that it was published in the *Austin Journal of Pharmacology and Therapeutics*, as well as in the *International Journal of Molecular Biology: Open Access*. A closer look at the paper shows that it contains a few suspicious elements. First, it talks about midichlorians, life forms that reside within the cells of all organisms and allow some beings to use The Force in the fantastic universe of the *Star Wars* franchise. It is also co-authored by Lucas McGeorge, whose name looks suspiciously like the director of the first *Star Wars* movie George Lucas. Indeed, the paper is a special type of prank, it was penned by a science blogger who wanted to expose how some predatory journals have such subpar peer-review standards that even the most ridiculous science-sounding articles have a chance of getting accepted (The Irish News 2017).

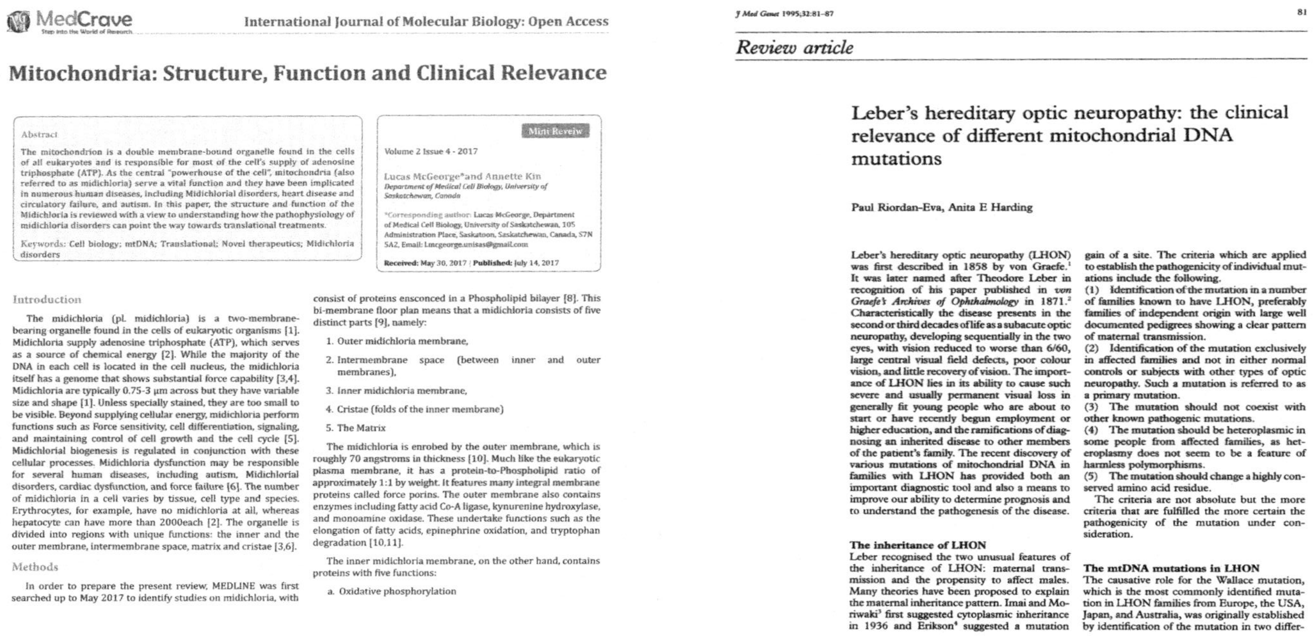

MedCrave
Step into the World of Research

International Journal of Molecular Biology: Open Access

Mitochondria: Structure, Function and Clinical Relevance

Abstract

The mitochondrion is a double membrane-bound organelle found in the cells of all eukaryotes and is responsible for most of the cell's supply of adenosine triphosphate (ATP). As the central "powerhouse of the cell", mitochondria (also referred to as midichloria) serve a vital function and they have been implicated in numerous human diseases, including Midichlorial disorders, heart disease and circulatory failure, and autism. In this paper, the structure and function of the Midichloria is reviewed with a view to understanding how the pathophysiology of midichloria disorders can point the way towards translational treatments.

Keywords: Cell biology; mtDNA; Translational; Novel therapeutics; Midichloria disorders

Mini Review

Volume 2 Issue 4 - 2017

Lucas McGeorge*and Annette Kin
Department of Medical Cell Biology, University of Saskatchewan, Canada

*Corresponding author: Lucas McGeorge, Department of Medical Cell Biology, University of Saskatchewan, 105 Administration Place, Saskatoon, Saskatchewan, Canada, S7N 5A2, Email: Lmcgeorge.unisas@gmail.com

Received: May 30, 2017 | Published: July 14, 2017

Introduction

The midichloria (pl. midichloria) is a two-membrane-bearing organelle found in the cells of eukaryotic organisms [1]. Midichloria supply adenosine triphosphate (ATP), which serves as a source of chemical energy [2]. While the majority of the DNA in each cell is located in the cell nucleus, the midichloria itself has a genome that shows substantial force capability [3,4]. Midichloria are typically 0.75-3 μm across but they have variable size and shape [1]. Unless specially stained, they are too small to be visible. Beyond supplying cellular energy, midichloria perform functions such as Force sensitivity, cell differentiation, signaling, and maintaining control of cell growth and the cell cycle [5]. Midichlorial biogenesis is regulated in conjunction with these cellular processes. Midichloria dysfunction may be responsible for several human diseases, including autism, Midichlorial disorders, cardiac dysfunction, and force failure [6]. The number of midichloria in a cell varies by tissue, cell type and species. Erythrocytes, for example, have no midichloria at all, whereas hepatocyte can have more than 2000each [2]. The organelle is divided into regions with unique functions: the inner and the outer membrane, intermembrane space, matrix and cristae [3,6].

Methods

In order to prepare the present review, MEDLINE was first searched up to May 2017 to identify studies on midichloria, with

consist of proteins ensconced in a Phospholipid bilayer [8]. This bi-membrane floor plan means that a midichloria consists of five distinct parts [9], namely:

1. Outer midichloria membrane,
2. Intermembrane space (between inner and outer membranes),
3. Inner midichloria membrane,
4. Cristae (folds of the inner membrane)
5. The Matrix

The midichloria is enrobed by the outer membrane, which is roughly 70 angstroms in thickness [10]. Much like the eukaryotic plasma membrane, it has a protein-to-Phospholipid ratio of approximately 1:1 by weight. It features many integral membrane proteins called force porins. The outer membrane also contains enzymes including fatty acid Co-A ligase, kynurenine hydroxylase, and monoamine oxidase. These undertake functions such as the elongation of fatty acids, epinephrine oxidation, and tryptophan degradation [10,11].

The inner midichloria membrane, on the other hand, contains proteins with five functions:

a. Oxidative phosphorylation

J Med Genet 1995;32:81-87 81

Review article

Leber's hereditary optic neuropathy: the clinical relevance of different mitochondrial DNA mutations

Paul Riordan-Eva, Anita E Harding

Leber's hereditary optic neuropathy (LHON) was first described in 1858 by von Graefe.[1] It was later named after Theodore Leber in recognition of his paper published in *von Graefe's Archives of Ophthalmology* in 1871.[2] Characteristically the disease presents in the second or third decades of life as a subacute optic neuropathy, developing sequentially in the two eyes, with vision reduced to worse than 6/60, large central visual field defects, poor colour vision, and little recovery of vision. The importance of LHON lies in its ability to cause such severe and usually permanent visual loss in generally fit young people who are about to start or have recently begun employment or higher education, and the ramifications of diagnosing an inherited disease to other members of the patient's family. The recent discovery of various mutations of mitochondrial DNA in families with LHON has provided both an important diagnostic tool and also a means to improve our ability to determine prognosis and to understand the pathogenesis of the disease.

The inheritance of LHON

Leber recognised the two unusual features of the inheritance of LHON: maternal transmission and the propensity to affect males. Many theories have been proposed to explain the maternal inheritance pattern. Imai and Moriwaki[3] first suggested cytoplasmic inheritance in 1936 and Erikson[4] suggested a mutation

gain of a site. The criteria which are applied to establish the pathogenicity of individual mutations include the following.

(1) Identification of the mutation in a number of families known to have LHON, preferably families of independent origin with large well documented pedigrees showing a clear pattern of maternal transmission.
(2) Identification of the mutation exclusively in affected families and not in either normal controls or subjects with other types of optic neuropathy. Such a mutation is referred to as a primary mutation.
(3) The mutation should not coexist with other known pathogenic mutations.
(4) The mutation should be heteroplasmic in some people from affected families, as heteroplasmy does not seem to be a feature of harmless polymorphisms.
(5) The mutation should change a highly conserved amino acid residue.

The criteria are not absolute but the more criteria that are fulfilled the more certain the pathogenicity of the mutation under consideration.

The mtDNA mutations in LHON

The causative role for the Wallace mutation, which is the most commonly identified mutation in LHON families from Europe, the USA, Japan, and Australia, was originally established by identification of the mutation in two differ-

FIGURE 10.2 Comparative front pages of two science articles.

It is telling that the paper, while it is written in relatively technical language, uses the language of biology, that medical students, taking part in the experiments, ought to be familiar with. Paper B is a legitimate science paper; it appears in a respectable journal and is authored by scientists, rather than film producers. The conclusions we can draw from these two experiments cannot be generalized too much. These are pedagogical experiments, not controlled social experiments. But we can draw some tentative conclusions. If a student is unable to recognize as unscientific a product that is written by an algorithm or a prankster, there is little hope that the average reader of science popularization, or possibly even a policy maker, could spot disinformation when it is rooted in pseudoscience.

The examples listed above are rather extreme, in the sense that they have not been created to really pass as science. I created the first bogus paper myself for pedagogical purposes, using the *mathgen* website, and the second bogus paper was created by a blogger to denounce predatory publishing. Proper pseudoscientific literature is instead produced to fool as many people as possible, it is usually created by pseudo-experts (more on this in the next section), and it can have several purposes. I will list a few:

a. **Promoting a product**. There is much pseudoscientific literature on homeopathy in predatory journals, which clearly helps feed a multibillion-euro industry worldwide.
b. **Sow doubt and stifle policy making**. Powerful interest groups disputed for a long time the strong scientific consensus that had formed around the dangers of smoking and global warming. Their fight was partly a PR operation and partly fuelled by creating a pseudoscientific literature to support unscientific claims (Oreskes and Conway 2010).
c. **Support an ideology with (pseudo)evidence**. The anti-vaccination movement has supported with pseudoscience a variety of claims over the years, including a link between the MMR vaccine and autism, and a link between vaccine adjuvants and autoimmune diseases.

I have argued that pseudoscience is hard to recognize. I have illustrated how easy it is to fall for products that look scientific but are not even closely related to proper science. One does not need to guess that properly constructed pseudoscience is much harder to debunk than the pedagogical examples I described above. Pseudoscientists are often people skilled in science talk and science methodology (Martini 2018). Pseudoscientists typically have what Collins and Evans (2008) call "interactional expertise", that is, the ability to speak and write in the language of scientists, and the knowledge of methodological and community practices in the field in which they are interactional experts.

Often interactional experts are people who previously worked in or close to the scientific community of reference. "Interactional expertise is mastery of the language of a domain, and mastery of any language, naturally occurring or specialist, requires enculturation within a linguistic community" (Collins and Evans 2008, 30). Interactional experts can easily pass for experts to any untrained eye, and that is how they produce writing and speech that looks scientific but is not the result of proper scientific research methods and practices (e.g. peer review). Interactional expertise is

> the ability to converse expertly about a practical skill or expertise, but without being able to practice it, learned through linguistic socialisation among the practitioners. Interactional expertise is exhibited by sociologists of scientific knowledge, by scientists themselves and by a large range of other actors.

It is in that category of "other actors" that one can find pseudoscientists.

The Language of Economic Experts

Nearly every science is exposed to the phenomenon of pseudoscience. There are contributing factors to the existence of pseudoscience: first, the technicality of the language; second, the complexity of the methodology; and third, how relevant a science is to policy or practical applications. The list may not be exhaustive. Some examples will clarify. Theoretical physics has an extremely high technical language, the methodology is rather simple (mathematical demonstrations and models) and the relevance to policy or applications is very limited. While it would be relatively easy to produce pseudoscience in theoretical physics, pseudo-physics is not very widespread. The incentives of producing pseudo-physics are limited and usually confined to the ramblings of eccentric individuals who think of themselves as ground-breaking maverick scientists. Similar considerations hold for historical and philological research because the limited applications that that kind of research produces make the existence of pseudo-philology a rare occasion. The exceptions, like *The Protocols of the Elders of Zion*, usually prove the rule: The protocols were tied to disinformation campaigns about Jews, promoted by antisemitic and Nazi propaganda – that is, ideological incentives (see, e.g., Bytwerk 2015).

Engineering has tremendous applications for practical purposes, so the incentives of producing pseudoscience in engineering are high. But engineering methodology is rather simple: "does it work?" Whatever application is produced by theory must bear immediately on observable phenomena. For instance, it might be technically challenging to measure the tensile strength of materials, say, in a bridge, or a skyscraper, but it is not a complex problem. The end results of engineering are straightforward to measure because any technical application of engineering is evaluated by its fitness for purpose – for example, whether the bridge will fall or stand.

In this chapter, I haven't talked much about economics so far. The rather long general preamble was necessary, but it is time to make amends. Let's have a look at economics vis-à-vis the three factors I mentioned at the beginning of this section.

A. **Economic language**. Given the impact of economic science on public life, we would expect economic communication to be simple. It is usually not. This is not a systematic review, yet some examples should illustrate. The next short extract is taken from the European Central Bank (ECB) *ECB staff macroeconomic projections for the euro area* (ECB 2022).

> … pressures are assessed to be more lasting than previously expected and to be only partly offset by dampening effects on growth from lower confidence and by weaker trade growth related to the conflict. […] in the absence of further upward shocks to commodity prices, energy inflation is projected to drop significantly over the projection horizon. In the short term, this decline relates to base effects, while the technical assumptions based on futures prices embed a decline in oil and wholesale gas prices resulting in a negligible contribution from the energy component to headline inflation in 2024.
>
> *(ECB 2022)*

The next extract is taken from an ING banking group's report:

> we expect 2023 to start with zero European Central Bank net bond purchases, and with the prospect of a 25bp hike within three months. As this prospect is roughly a year away, it has allowed EUR interest rates to take a more sanguine view of the global inflation groundswell. Some of it is justified by slower price dynamics than in the rest of the world, but tightening steps by other central banks, in particular the Federal Reserve, have the potential to focus minds in EUR markets.
>
> *(ING 2021)*

Both extracts are meant for professionals, most likely policy makers, investors and businesses. That is a broader public than the in-group of professional economists, yet a narrower group than the general public. The language is technical as well as metaphorical and at times colourful, more so in the latter document (ING 2021), while the ECB (2022) uses drier language, possibly because its audience is less business oriented: "the economy is largely a rhetorical affair" (McCloskey, this volume). We can imagine an audience of laypeople trying to tell the difference between an economic article, based on research, models, statistics and logical arguments, and another document that someone with interactional expertise in economics may write without any backing from argumentation or empirical data. I venture to guess that the general public's ability to tell economics from pseudo-economics would fare worse than the students that take part in my pedagogical experiments.

B. **Economic methodology**. Going into the details of this aspect would probably take too long to address it properly in the space of this chapter. I take it that it is rather commonsensical and an accepted truism in the economic community that economic calculations are neither simple nor straightforward. The effects of economic policies are not as easily measurable as the tensile strength of a suspension bridge's cables. Economic policies affect a wide range of social and economic aspects, many of which are interdependent. It is telling that for even extremely well-studied episodes in economic history like the *Great Depression,* there are several competing theories that try to explain its causes. In short, while the engineer is easily proven wrong when the bridge they designed collapses, being right or wrong in economics is a complex affair, not easily established by facts.

C. **Relevance to policy**. Among the social sciences, economics is the one that has the strongest presence in the public arena. Economists have the policy makers' ears and economic science controls a wide range of policy analysis. It is easy to argue that there are very strong incentives for pseudo-economics to exist.

Economics has a highly specialized language, a complex methodology, and strong incentives towards the production of economic "knowledge" at a cost cheaper than that of proper economic research and analysis. This is a combination of factors that any attempt to make economic public should take into account. Economic communication is not likely to exist in isolation from numerous attempts by pseudo-economists to drive alternative economic narratives to the public.

Clearly, in economics, there aren't only good economists and pseudo-economists. There is plenty of disagreement in economics and surely different schools of thought think of the opposite side as pseudoscience. This is however just rhetorical manoeuvring to discredit intellectual opponents. While some parts of economic science might be built on stronger foundations than others, an economic paper that has falsified historical accounts, or manipulated data, should be counted as pseudoscientific, regardless of the economic camp one finds more convincing. There are several markers of pseudoscience: they are neither necessary nor sufficient criteria for identifying a text or speech as pseudoscientific, but they function as red flags. The more red flags one finds in an output, the more we should suspect we are in front of a case of pseudoscience.

An account of these markers of expertise and, conversely, pseudo-expertise would be beyond the scope of this chapter (but see Martini 2019; Martini and Andreoletti 2021), but let us have a look at some examples.

- In the absence of peer review or informal evaluation from peers, an article does not hold the same degree of authoritativeness, it could be the scientist's opinion, but established conclusions are almost always reached by a certain degree of consensus within a community of researchers.
- The presence of biases is a red flag because it might signal advocacy rather than inquiry. The scientists tied to particular industries or interest groups that played a role in the climate change debates were doing mostly advocacy, and quite little scientific inquiry (Kitcher 2010).

- A mismatch between the field of expertise of the author and the relevant field of expertise of a science-looking product is also a red flag because experts gain their knowledge in relatively narrow fields of specialization, and it is unlikely someone will be a competent epistemic authority in, say, quantum physics, oncology and geopolitics. Polymaths are a rarity, and we should at the very least question their status if we think we found one.

These are, of course, only some examples; much more can be said about identifying experts and pseudo-experts. What is important to note is that it is a fallible enterprise but an important one. Because there are many levels of expertise and specialization, red flags cannot decide the truth of the matter, but they can and most likely will point us in the right direction when adjudicating an expert's epistemological worth.

Conclusion

In this chapter, I raised a problem for any attempt to communicate economics to the public. Such attempt must deal with the problem of pseudo-economics. Public communicators of science do not only have the challenge of simplifying scientific discourse without oversimplifying it but also that of competing with pseudoscience for attention and trust. Not all sciences are equally subject to such competitive distortions, but I have argued that economics is. That is because of its highly technical language, its complex methodology, and the strong incentives to produce pseudo-economic literature. To be sure, there are not only two distinct camps: one populated by good economists and the other populated by quacks. There are most likely better and worse economic theories, predictions and explanations. But there will very likely be a significant amount of literature that would be disqualified as unscientific or pseudoscientific by any trained eye, and yet look trustworthy in the eyes of a layperson. This literature is muddying the waters of economic communication, begging the questions "who are the economic experts?" and "how can one tell?"

Note

The two genuine science papers whose images were shown in the text are as follows:

Novikov, R. G., & Santacesaria, M. (2013). Monochromatic reconstruction algorithms for two-dimensional multi-channel inverse problems. *International Mathematics Research Notices*, 2013(6), 1205–1229.

Riordan-Eva, P., & Harding, A. E. (1995). Leber's hereditary optic neuropathy: The clinical relevance of different mitochondrial DNA mutations. *Journal of Medical Genetics*, 32(2), 81.

Digging Deeper

Discussion Questions

1. Which kind(s) of expert do you trust most and why?
2. Which field(s) of expertise do you trust most and why?

Suggested Further Reading

Reiss, J. (2020). Why do experts disagree? *Critical Review*, 32(1–3), 218–241.

Note

1 https://thatsmathematics.com/mathgen/ Last accessed April 30, 2022.

References

Bytwerk, R. L. (2015). Believing in "Inner Truth": The protocols of the elders of Zion in Nazi Propaganda, 1933–1945. *Holocaust and Genocide Studies*, 29(2), 212–229.

Collins, H., & Evans, R. (2008). *Rethinking expertise.* University of Chicago Press.

European Central Bank. (2022). ECB staff macroeconomic projections for the euro area. ISSN 2529-4466, QB-CE-22-001-EN-N. URL: https://www.ecb.europa.eu/pub/projections/html/ecb.projections202203_ecbstaff~44f998dfd7.en.html (Accessed April 2022).

ING. (2021). Rates Outlook: The eurozone still has a long way to go. *ING Economic and Financial Analysis.* December 9, 2021. URL: https://think.ing.com/articles/rates-outlook-eurozone-still-a-long-way-to-go (Accessed April 2022).

Kitcher, P. (2010). The climate change debates. *Science*, 328(5983), 1230–1234.

Martini, C. (2018). Ad hominem arguments, rhetoric, and science communication. *Studies in Logic, Grammar and Rhetoric*, 55(1), 151–166.

Martini, C. (2019). The epistemology of expertise. In: Fricker, M., Graham, P. J., Henderson, D., and Pedersen, N. J. L. L. (Eds.), *The Routledge handbook of social epistemology.* Routledge, 115–122.

Martini, C., & Andreoletti, M. (2021). Genuine versus bogus scientific controversies: The case of statins. *History and Philosophy of the Life Sciences*, 43(4), 1–23.

Online Source 1. (2012). That's Mathematics! URL: https://thatsmathematics.com/blog/mathgen/ (Accessed April 2022).

Oreskes, N., & Conway, E. M. (2010). *Merchants of doubt: How a handful of scientists obscured the truth on issues from tobacco smoke to global warming.* Bloomsbury Publishing.

Tetlock, P. E. (2005). *Expert political judgment.* Princeton University Press.

The Irish News. (2017). A blogger fooled three scientific journals into publishing a fake *Star Wars*-themed paper. *The Irish News.* July 24, 2017. URL: https://www.irishnews.com/magazine/science/2017/07/24/news/a-blogger-fooled-three-scientific-journals-into-publishing-a-fake-star-wars-themed-paper-1091631/ (Accessed April 2022).

11

ETHICAL CONSIDERATIONS IN MAKING ECONOMICS PUBLIC

Joan Leach and Fabien Medvecky

Introduction

Communication always and necessarily involves social interactions, and these usually come with a healthy dose of ethical and moral challenges. Communicating economics is no exception. In fact, because economics is so deeply engrained in how we perform social interactions and make social decisions, communicating economics has a double dose of ethical challenges. This chapter will centre around the discussion on a funny dance found throughout economics. Open any economics textbook, and within the first few pages, you'll come across a section about the distinction between *positive* and *normative* analysis in economics, the former being largely descriptive analyses of economic systems and the latter being value-laden assessments of such systems. In this chapter, we want to draw out how this distinction plays a particularly important role in ethical considerations for making economics public. The communication of economics is especially pertinent given economics is both socially very powerful (it dictates much of our life), and it is about the social world; economics is a social science.

Economics as a social science is a funny beast. It's unquestioningly a social science; its objects of study are social phenomena and interactions. Yet it also sits apart from other social sciences, intellectually, methodologically, and structurally. Structurally, economics departments increasingly sit in business schools or divisions rather than in social science ones; methodologically, as both Leontief and Friedman have noted, economics is often more concerned with the mathematical models than with the empirical content that this modelling is supposed to represent (Friedman, 1999; Leontief, 1982); and intellectually, economists are the only social scientists who hold a majority view that interdisciplinary knowledge is not better than knowledge obtained by a single discipline (Fourcade et al., 2015). Moreover, there is quite some level of consensus and agreement

DOI: 10.4324/9781003283447-15

between economists, but the views shared are very different with that of non-economists; in fact, the more economists agree among themselves on a point, the more their view is distant from the public perspective on the same point (Sapienza & Zingales, 2013). There is a significant gap in perspectives between society—the object economists as social scientists—and economists themselves. Before launching into considerations of some of the ethical issues that arise when communicating economics, we want to highlight two distinctions that are foundational for the discussion.

Firstly, as has already been noted in previous chapters, there is a distinction between economics (the social science discipline) and the economy (the artefact or object). Of course, economics studies the economy, but economics studies much more than that. It also studies individual behaviour (sometimes in the economy, but not necessarily), it studies models of markets (not all of which sit with the economy), and more besides. Perhaps one way to think of the relationship between economics and the economy is as analogous to science and nature. Science sometimes studies nature, but other times, it studies models of what could be (such as theoretical physics), it studies the 'individual behaviour' of chemicals (sometimes as found in nature, sometimes not, such as when creating new compounds), and more besides. So while much of this volume has been very focused on economics (the discipline) rather than the economy, we will be drawing on both the distinction between the two and the interaction between them.

Secondly, there is a distinction between normative and positive economics. Classically, the distinction distinguishes between the *positive*, statement (or testing) of facts, the *what is* of economics, and the *normative* statement of values, the *what should be* of economics. For Perloff, *positive* statements are "a testable hypothesis about cause and effects" while *normative* statements are "a conclusion as to whether something is good or bad" (Perloff, 2007). Positive economic analysis, then, is the science-like, empirical type of economics, and normative economic analysis is the philosophical, value-laden analysis that ensues. The distinction is presumed to be clean, and a common claim in almost every economics textbook is that "economics is about positive analysis which measures the costs and benefits of different course of action" (Hubbard et al., 2012). This commonly accepted distinction, we argue, is unrealistic, and this adds a layer of ethical complexity to communicating economics.

Learning from the Ethics of Science Communicating When Making Economics Public

Positive economics is presented as a science-like form of economics; it has the universalisable, detached accuracy of empirical claims. It is the fact-based economic knowledge we hold, from the effects of price elasticity on the distribution of taxes to the effect of decreasing unemployment on inflation. Being fact-based gives positive economics something like the epistemic authority of science; these are statements that we should take to have a higher level of credibility than most statements, just like scientific claims. And communicating these claims also shares the ethical challenges familiar to communicating scientific claims. We draw on that existing literature to think through some of the challenges for making economics public.

Drawing on issues from science communication when thinking about the ethics of communicating positive economics is, as an economist might put it, efficient. Much of the work has already been done; it's largely a case of looking at what has been said about the ethics of communicating science and then using a 'find and replace' function, especially if we take economics to be primarily concerned with the positive economics side of the discipline. Thinking of economics solely in terms of positive claims and analysis is neat; it's epistemically clean. It separates what can be known from all the mess of value-driven claims and analyses. Ironically, it also separates what can be known from what matters and what is important, since 'mattering' and 'being important' are normative statements. But here's the catch: positive economics largely studies things that do matter *because* they matter—there's a normative moment in deciding what is studied—so pretending the normative can be separated from the positive is nigh impossible.

A well-rehearsed ethical issue in science communication is how one might balance informing and persuading, along with the effects of one of the communication's more favoured tools: storytelling (and the challenge of accuracy in storytelling) (Dahlstrom & Ho, 2012; Spahn, 2012). Let's begin with persuasion that a discussion of the ethics of economics communication is even legible or possible is, in great part, due to the ground-breaking work of Deirdre McCloskey's *The Rhetoric of Economics*. In that book, she makes the point that "economics is literary." While she didn't mean that the writing style of economists is on par with that of the novelists, she emphatically makes the point that economics "was literary, like physics or mathematics or biology, a persuasive realm where the work was done by human arguments, not godlike Proof." McCloskey goes on to show that economists' adoption of scientific rhetoric to persuade is one of the major achievements of contemporary academic economics. That is not to say that economic writers are untruthful or fabulators, rather it is that they are writing with intent—the intent to persuade.

Persuasion takes on many forms including word choice, style of argumentation, preferred modes of evidence, and the framing of arguments around certain issues while leaving other issues in relative neglect. The economist and Nobel Prize winner Paul Krugman (2020, p. 5), for example, points out that for much of his career, he thought that he was engaged in straightforward positive economics—doing the analysis and collecting the evidence on trends, global patterns of trade, the location, and outcomes of various industries. He saw this work as not intended to persuade, to have specific policy outcomes, or to be political in any way. However, he now says that "in some cases, even asking certain questions has become a partisan act." Furthermore, he argues that "in many cases, accepting what the evidence says about an economic question will be seen as a partisan act ... simply recognising reality became seen as a liberal position." As distressed as he is that politics has overrun his discipline, he acknowledges that at some level, the questions asked in economics are about values, and those values can be more or less polarised and more or less the subtext for persuasion, political or otherwise.

The key issue is not that economics is rhetorical; every bit of human communication is rhetorical in that it invents and styles forms of argument; this includes proof-making in mathematics and quantitative economics even when the audience for such arguments is vanishingly small. The key issue is that with the acknowledgement of economic rhetorics comes a series of ethical questions for both the rhetor and the audience.

One of the key rhetorical-ethical moments for any field is how rhetors present their arguments in narrative form. In short, it is the question of "what kind of story is this?" For economists, for example, one powerful narrative is the story of a 'trend' in data—prices rising, employment falling, and the locus of economic power shifting over time or geography. The drive to tell a story in 'trend' terms is powerful, and there are significant meta-scientific questions with an ethical dimension at play—how many data points are needed to talk about a trend? When a 'trend' is identified, what does a rhetor do with data points outside the trend line—are they 'anomalies' or part of the story or are they explained away? The 'trend' storyline is so persuasive in public economic rhetoric that trend narratives are the starting point for public engagement with economics. Textbooks routinely introduce economic data in 'three core trends.' Trend rhetoric in economics quickly crosses over the positive and normative economic traditions. Trends are both collections of data (positive) and directions that are being taken that imply certain ends (normative).

Another familiar issue in the ethics of science communication is around hype, cover-up, and timing. The kairotic element of economic rhetoric, perhaps, raises the most public ethics challenge for economics. Kairos, or the element of 'timing,' raises ethical issues of expectation, and the timing of an economic analysis has the potential to change the future in powerful ways. This is not the least because the dynamics of economic developments are famously subject to consumer expectations. A key example is the price of gold (Beckert, 2015). Analysts frequently make predictions about the gold price that can encourage investors to buy gold, thus increasing its price. Gold's reputation as a 'crisis currency' only makes the timing effects of economic forecasting more sensitive. Merely telling investors that gold prices are rising can cause concern.

The corollary of this timing issue is a certain 'hype,' for example about some investments. Technological innovation is an area especially sensitive to timing and hype. Innovations need to be credible for investors to be interested in them, but they also need to be novel and offer new possibilities. Thus, there is substantial rhetorical pressure for technologies to be 'hyped' by presenting optimal future scenarios precisely at the moment that investors might want them most. These future scenarios drive behaviour and the direction of markets and sometimes confound the rational expectations of economists.

This brings up a last ethical challenge we want to consider, one that is especially pertinent to economics—reflexivity. We follow Thompson in taking it that reflexivity "occurs when the use of a theory or instrument affects or alters the phenomena it has been introduced to observe and explain" (Thompson, 2017). As has been noted by MacKenzie and others, "economists affect markets by saying what markets are doing" (MacKenzie et al., 2007; Muniesa et al., 2007). Above, we mention expectation as a primer for the reflexivity of economics, and there is, perhaps, no clearer example of the role that expectation plays in shaping economic systems than the revision of the original Phillips curve (that, roughly, asserts an inverse relationship between the rates of unemployment and inflation) into the 'expectation-augmented Phillips curve,' where the expectation of a rise in inflation is taken to have a measurable effect. What is often left out of this revision is that the expectation that inflation will rise is not unrelated to what economists forecast or state about *their* expectations or the forecast of *their* models. And economics is reflexive beyond 'expectations' and 'the making of markets.' What economics studies (the questions that are asked), how economics studies them (the methods and assumptions that go into answering those questions), and what economists say about these (how these answers are communicated) all shape the very object that is studied. This brings a very unique set of ethical concerns for making economics public. Communicating economics is always performative in a reflexive way: the communication of economics not only brings forth information, knowledge, and perspective but also creates or brings into being (in a very real way) a specific world, namely the world it assumes and imagines.

Wrapping It Up

Returning to the positive economics and science analogy, a similar challenge to the positive–normative distinction has been noted about science; science is always imbued with normativity. Indeed, "[v]alues and judgements appear in the questions researchers choose to ask, in the way they choose to answer these questions, and in many other ways besides" (Medvecky & Leach, 2019, p. 18). Many scientists take the more common (and coherent) response and acknowledge that while normative judgements are littered throughout, the *results* are as objective as can be (Gray & Campbell, 2009). We might say the same for positive economic analyses; there's normativity throughout, but the results are as objective as can be. Although that claim is more difficult for economics than for much of science. Laying aside or bracketing questions of value when studying unemployment seems to miss the point of why we study unemployment and can't be compared to laying aside questions of value when studying the polarity of molecules. The normative assumptions we make as to why we study unemployment matter: are we interested because of the effect unemployment has on people's welfare or because of the effect unemployment has on GDP? Indeed, concerns over the appropriateness of treating economics as if the normative claims could be neatly separated from the positive claims have led to a significant pushback, most notably by students (and some educators) of economics around the globe, from *The Econocracy* to the *CORE e*-textbook project (which, we note, doesn't mention the positive–normative distinction) (Earle et al., 2016).

Alongside other authors in this book, we note that economics, as a discipline, is quite a novice at making itself public. The good news is that it can draw on existing work around the ethics of making public (particularly the ethics of science communication). But economics also faces some unique ethical challenges, most notably from the common (but largely false) narrative that positive claims can be neatly parsed from normative claims. Revising our assumption of a positive–normative distinction in favour of recognising positive–normative blurring helps anyone engaged in making economics public to notice important ethical concerns. From the style of argument that we take to the story we tell, to the world we imagine—and bring into being through communication, through setting expectations, through presenting—there will be normativity. If we hold democratic aspirations, we need to find the right balance between engaging with the positive(ish) claims while also allowing and empowering people to question and engage with the normative claims.

Digging Deeper

Discussion Questions

1. How real and how realistic is the normative/positive distinction?
2. What harm might it have done to how economics is communicated?

Suggested Further Reading

Hands, D. W. (2012). The positive-normative dichotomy and economics. In U. Maki. (Ed.), *Handbook of the philosophy of science* (pp. 219–239). Elsevier and North Holland.
Małecka, M. (2021). Values in economics: a recent revival with a twist. *Journal of Economic Methodology, 28*(1), 88–97.

References

Beckert, J. (2015). How fictional expectations drive the dynamics of economic developments. *Max Planck Institute for the Study of Societies.* Retrieved from https://www.mpg.de/9354212/fictional-expectations-economic-developments.
Dahlstrom, M. F., & Ho, S. S. (2012). Ethical considerations of using narrative to communicate science. *Science Communication, 34*(5), 592–617.
Earle, J., Moran, C., & Ward-Perkins, Z. (2016). *The econocracy: the perils of leaving economics to the experts.* Manchester University Press.

Fourcade, M., Ollion, E., & Algan, Y. (2015). The superiority of economists. *Journal of Economic Perspectives, 29*(1), 89–114.

Friedman, M. (1999). Conversation with Milton Friedman. In B. Snowdon, & H. R. Vane (Eds.), *Conversations with leading economists*. Edward Elgar, 124–144.

Gray, N. J., & Campbell, L. M. (2009). Science, policy advocacy, and marine protected areas. *Conservation Biology, 23*(2), 460–468.

Hubbard, G., Garnett, A., & Lewis, P. (2012). *Essentials of economics*. Pearson Higher Education AU.

Krugman, P. (2020). *Arguing with zombies: economics, politics, and the fight for a better future*. W. W. Norton and Company, New York.

Leontief, W. (1982). Academic economics. *Science, 217*(4555), 104–107.

MacKenzie, D., Muniesa, F., & Siu, L. (2007). Introduction. In MacKenzie, D., Muniesa, F., & Siu, L, (Eds.), Do economists make markets. In *On the performativity of economics*. Princeton University Press, 1–19.

Medvecky, F., & Leach, J. (2019). *An ethics of science communication*. Springer Nature.

Muniesa, F., Millo, Y., & Callon, M. (2007). An introduction to market devices. *The Sociological Review, 55*(2_suppl), 1–12.

Perloff, J. (2007). *Microeconomics*, 4th ed. Pearson Education.

Sapienza, P., & Zingales, L. (2013). Economic experts versus average Americans. *American Economic Review, 103*(3), 636–642.

Spahn, A. (2012). And lead us (not) into persuasion…? Persuasive technology and the ethics of communication. *Science and Engineering Ethics, 18*(4), 633–650.

Thompson, P. B. (2017). *The spirit of the soil: agriculture and environmental ethics*. Routledge.

SECTION FOUR

Economics in a Democratic World

We close in the grandest way, with an overview of the political and the powerful, arguing that politics, economics and communication are inseparable. Not only is it not possible to separate them – economics is a form of communication – we shouldn't want to separate them. If we aspire to something like liberal democracies, then we need space and capacity for free economic talk.

A (probably the) foundational voice on the social life of economics, Deirdre Nansen McCloskey – makes a grand argument linking economic action to rhetoric and beyond that to freedom and governing. In this piece, she argues for a humane liberalism that understands markets as constituted by words and deeds and a political culture that seeks to respect words and doubts. 'Markets', she argues, 'live on people's tongues, which, therefore, must be free to wag'. This is an exciting and provocative way to end a chapter that sees ancient Greeks and Steve Jobs, politics and economics and 'sweet talk' as all within the same frame.

What our authors have written throughout this volume, we hope, is only an opening, an invitation to thought and a provocation to action. Not only markets, but the discipline of economics too, should live on people's tongues and be free – and empowered – to wag.

DOI: 10.4324/9781003283447-16

12

FREE SPEECH, RHETORIC, AND A FREE ECONOMY[1]

Deirdre Nansen McCloskey

Free Speech Supports a Free Economy and Vice Versa

Adam Smith the *ur*-liberal declared in 1762–1763 in his *Lectures on Jurisprudence*,

> The offering of a shilling, which to us appears to have so plain and simple a meaning, is in reality offering an argument to persuade someone to do so and so as it is for his interest. ... And in this manner everyone is practicing oratory on others through the whole of his life.
>
> *(Smith 1978, 1982 [1762–1763, 1766]. Report of 1762-3 vi. 56, p. 352)*

Yes. The market is a form of persuasion, sweet talk. The practice of oratory, persuasion, and the changing of minds by speech accounts in a modern economy such as that of the U.S. for fully a quarter of labor income (Klamer and McCloskey 1995). The liberal theory of speech, therefore, strongly parallels the liberal theory of the market.

Rhetoric and liberty are doubly linked. For one thing, any defense of liberty will make use of rhetoric, "rhetoric" understood as "speaking with persuasive intent instead of using physical violence." For another, the free market in ideas is a rhetorical idea at the heart of free societies. The evidence for the second proposition—that liberty is rhetorical, a matter of sweet talk, is not so persuasive as that defenses of liberty are themselves rhetorical. If true, however, the proposition that liberty is rhetorical is more important. The growth of knowledge may justify a constitution of liberty, as the economist and philosopher Friedrich Hayek believed, but rhetoric gives persuasive tongue to both liberty and knowledge. Free speech is more than merely parallel to free exchange. A liberal society is the one that gets its rhetoric straight.

DOI: 10.4324/9781003283447-17

For a long time now, of course, intellectuals have been trying to avoid "mere" rhetoric, even in defense of liberty. They declare that they depend only on logic and just facts, Ma'am. Their defenses are commonly set in the axiom-and-proof rhetoric of the line Euclid–Descartes–Hobbes–Russell. Formality is trumps, and the meaning of "formality" is an imitation of Euclid's certitude. Especially in the intersection of economics and politics, the formality is often false and is easily denied.

A more political and Western definition of liberty, due again to Aristotle, is the condition of being the citizen of a polis in which the citizens, political animals, take turns ruling. Rousseau likewise defines civil liberty as obeying laws that the people themselves had formulated. But this civic-liberty definition reduces liberty to obeying democratic rulers, which is paradoxical—free to obey—and seemed to Mill and Tocqueville to be dangerous.

A similar problem—and here I come to the nub of the issue—arises with various other sorts of such "positive" liberty, the liberty to do such-and-such. Positive liberty is good in itself since it is good that people are enabled to do what they wish, at any rate if what they want is not something like "murder all Jews." But transfers making some people richer will of course violate other people's liberty defined in the same way.

J. S. Mill was inconsistent, as many modern theorists have been, in combining a budding enthusiasm for positive liberty with a fear of coercively democratic opinion damaging individual liberty. Isaiah Berlin (1969 [1958], to which further reference is made) made persuasive arguments for confining the liberty word to "negative" liberty, liberty-from, as against the positive liberty-to.

The contrasts among the definitions of liberty are plainer if translated into terms of coercion. On what grounds does Mr. Brown claim the right to coerce Ms. Jones, if Brown is her husband or an employer or an IRS agent? For the ancients, and for the theorists of modern democracy and socialism, the grounds of coercion are mere membership in a community—a family, polis, church, nation, or social class. Such a social contract may be a lovely thing, but one has to admit that it gives ample grounds for coercion to achieve positive "liberty."

For us old-fashioned or European-style liberals, or humane American real liberals 2.0, the grounds are far too wide. A private person, we all say, is simply not to be coerced. As Lincoln noted in 1864,

> With some the word liberty may mean for each man to do as he pleases, with himself, and with the product of his labor; while with others the same word may mean for some men to do as they please with other men, and the product of other men's labor.

The coercive power of the slave-owner is the same as that of the tax eater, the positive liberty to violate the negative liberty of others.

Economic liberty defined in this negative way parallels good rhetoric. The notion is that liberty is at the bottom, a condition of un-coerced persuasion, the right to say no. One could assert, as the philosopher P. H. Partridge (1967), for example, does, following many anti-rhetoricians, that "un-coerced" entails "un-manipulated." The low standing of rhetoric after Dr. Goebbels brings such possibilities to mind. One imagines a right of a free man to un-manipulated opinions, a world free from beer commercials and sound bites, free from dishonest appeals to "build a Mexican wall" and free from governmental programs for bringing children up as patriots.

But the criterion is too broad to be properly assigned to liberty. If the manipulation is physical, not verbal, then it does constrain liberty. If Goebbels imprisons his enemies he is depriving them of liberty. If, on the other hand, he merely talks persuasively to them, even lies to them, or even runs a splendid film about Nazi successes in the Berlin Olympics in their presence, he is not in a useful sense engaged in "coercion." Michael (as against Charles) Taylor has argued that "coercion" must be confined to physical action or to "the successful making of credible, substantial threats" backed by physical coercion (1982, 11–21, especially 19–20, 147). Otherwise, it is "merely" rhetoric. Sticks and stones/May break my bones/But names can never hurt me. To call a heated argument "verbal rape" is to demean actual victims of physical rape.

One more restriction on the notion of "coercion" is required if "liberty" is to mean what it says. Consider the Paradox of Bread. Question: Is not my buying of a loaf of bread an infringement of the liberty of another, namely, the liberty to buy the loaf of bread "free of restraint by another person"? If I buy the loaf, the price is made a tiny bit higher. Though the bit is tiny, it affects all who buy the bread, and so the loss of "liberty" in total, summed over all the other millions of buyers of bread, is just the price I pay for the loaf. That's economics.

There is no question that it is a constraint. The higher price does constrain others to buy less bread (in particular, they can't buy the loaf I myself bought) or less of other things (since I take some of the social output for my own consumption). "Men are largely interdependent," noted Berlin, "and no man's activity is so completely private as never to obstruct the lives of others in any way" (124; cf. 155; and for an economist making the same point, Knight 1929, 4n: "bargains between individuals usually have effects, good or bad, for persons other than the immediate parties"). No man is an island entirely of itself.

To solve the Paradox of Bread—the Paradox being that if "coercion" is extended so far, then no one is permitted to do anything that would affect anyone else, ever—one must draw the line of coercion, I would assert, at dyadic coercion, one person (physically) coercing another, directly. Universal coercion would be required to stop all indirect coercion. In practical political terms, if every claim of damage by Jones's economic activity were honored, no economic action would be possible, unless by perfect lump-sum taxes (as we say in the Department of Economics), redistributing the pure gains from trade.

What, though, about lies, propaganda, false advertising, hate speech and all that is nasty in rhetoric? Aren't these "coercion"? What of Plato's ancient charge:

"And won't whoever does this artfully make the same thing appear to the same people sometimes just and some time, when he prefers, unjust?" (*Phaedrus* 361d in Plato 1997, 538)? Or "the sophist isn't one of the people who know but is one of the people who imitate" (*Sophist* 267E in Plato 1997, 292).

Behind the demand that opinion be "un-manipulated" by speech sits a demand that the speech is True. Truth, however, cannot and should not be guaranteed by the official power of the government. In an NBC news broadcast on 25 June 1990, the reporter was vexed that he could not see the truth shining out from the claims and counterclaims for biodegradable plastic. The manufacturer he interviewed claimed that the plastic degrades in dumps. The environmentalist he interviewed scoffed at the very idea. What gives the (weak) guarantee of approaching small-t truth is that we encourage people to listen, really listen, with philosophical sophistication about essences and rhetorical sophistication about form.

One must of course draw a line at fraud. Proving fraud requires only, as Gorgias says (to a Socrates sneering at the very idea), merely "the persuasion … that takes place in law courts" (*Gorgias* 454b in Plato 1997, 799), not the insight into God's Truth that Plato/Socrates always demands. If the manufacturer does not honestly believe that plastic bags with corn starch pellets introduced into the manufacturing do in truth degrade at the dump—for example, we catch him sending an internal email in which he proposes knowingly to make the fraudulent claim—and yet in his advertising calls his product "Eco-Safe," then the government's power in the form of court action might be appropriate. Yet a story debunking the claim on the evening news would do as good a job with less threat to liberty. If the sale or argument is not fraudulent (the lawyers could help us understand what in detail the word might mean), then there is no further case against "manipulation." Otherwise, any offer of sale and any use of argument would have to be accounted "manipulation," Darwin "manipulating" his audience to believe in evolution by natural selection, say.

The notion of "manipulation," in short, is terminally muddy. It has always been anti-rhetorical. Partridge imagined people un-manipulated by rich newspaper owners or cunning advertisers. Yet the government is the only referee available if rhetoric is to be graded and passed, officially. It is the only "we" available to assure that "we" get the truth. The political rhetoric matters. How we talk about the government sets the limits within which it works. We get the government we talk about. It was the rhetoric of early nineteenth-century liberalism that limited the government, not limited in Russia or China at the time. Thomas Macaulay wrote in 1830,

> Government, as government … carries on controversy, not with reasons, but with threats and bribes. If it employs reasons, it does so, not in virtue of any powers which belong to it as government. Thus, instead of a contest between argument and argument, we have a contest between argument and force.
>
> *([1830] 1881, 165)*

Macaulay and I favor the argument.

Rhetoric Is Not Merely Bullshit, and Saying So Kills Liberalism

The ideological postulate has poisoned even scientific conversation. The postulate is well expressed by Partridge (1967):

> In modern societies manipulation in various forms is at least as important
> as the processes we normally identify as coercive. It is well known that,
> within a society, a group of men may enjoy such control over property
> or the means of production, or over an educational system or the media
> of communication, that they are able to determine within a fairly narrow
> range the alternatives between which their fellow citizens can choose.
>
> *(223)*

Partridge knows for sure that the postulate entails an active government to deliver "freedom from want" and "freedom from fear" (224, col. 1) and now "freedom from rhetoric."

But the postulate is empirically faulty. It embodies a notion that communication is unusually persuasive in the modern world, that governmental propaganda
works, and that advertising is what keeps us all rich by having us run on a squirrel's
treadmill of consumption. Journalists and other media personalities like to introduce themselves as a new and all-powerful corps of persuaders. But in fact, the
greeklings who listened to wily Odysseus in council were no less under the spell of
language. Humans just are. There is nothing particularly modern about the spell of
persuasion, for good or ill. To see one's children watching advertising on television,
and to see them develop through ages 3–12 from gullibility to disappointment to
skepticism and finally to sarcasm, is to become educated in the limits of false persuasion. The endlessly prospering television program *Saturday Night Live* lives on
raucous satire about its own medium, appealing most to the television generation.

The trouble with philosophical claims to assure the Truth is that the only alternative to persuasion is direct coercion. Exaggerating the power of persuasion
is the first step toward replacing persuasion with coercion. The attacks on advertising in the United States since the 1920s have yielded a widespread opinion that
advertising is magically powerful, and that, therefore, the government must step
in to tell us what is true. But if advertising were as powerful as J. K. Galbraith
and Vance Packard claimed, then the advertisers would of course be fabulously
rich. The frequent failures of both the Allied and Axis propaganda machines,
even when not offsetting each other with claims and counterclaims, suggest that
people are in fact less gullible than the critics of commercial free speech believe.
Propaganda about the nature of man under socialism did not persuade Eastern
Europeans, despite a four-decade run through every means of rhetoric (and in
Russia, seven decades).

Manipulation is oversold. That is good news, because, to repeat, there is no
acceptable alternative in a free society to persuasion. Likewise, I am suggesting,
in markets. My colleague Ralph Cintron points to rhetoric as a "storehouse of

social energy," inspiring people (again, for good or ill) to this or that action. He and I agree deeply that the energetics of rhetoric is unpredictable because speech is, that is, its danger and its creativity. Likewise in the economy. The economy does not work through capital (McCloskey 2016). It works through discovery of a better way. Thus free speech.

The alternative to persuasion is displayed in Thucydides' dialogue at Melos, in which the Melians try to use the conventions of persuasion with the now all-powerful Athenians. The Athenians, though claiming the ethical high ground of a free people governed by persuasion, spurn the Melians' attempt to use the Athenians' own theory to defend themselves from brute force. We are the stronger, the Athenian delegation notes, in the style of vulgar (and even not so vulgar) Marxians. So shut up. Surrender or die. The Melians do not surrender, and in the next season of campaigning the Athenians kill all the men and sell the women and children into slavery. The refusal of the Athenians to enter a persuasive discourse that they themselves had invented signaled their decay (White 1984, 76–80).

There are only three possibilities. Either you have been persuaded of something or you have been coerced or you have not considered the question at all and have adopted whatever opinion springs first to mind. The free person resists coercion and spurns unconsidered opinion. Berlin quotes a revealing dilemma put by Comte, who like Plato and the rest in the anti-rhetorical tradition was quite certain he had his hands on the eternal absolute: "If we do not allow free thinking in chemistry or biology, why should we allow it in morals or politics?" Why indeed? It is what is wrong with the notion that we can ascertain a Truth which all must obey. We are right to try to persuade each other and right to ask for an audience. But we are not right to contemplate "allowing" free thought and speech, as "allowing" free trade and innovation, as some sort of entertaining luxury inessential to our lives.

As Berlin pointed out, Comte's question exposes the rot in political rationalism—that is, in Platonism:

> first, that all men have one true purpose; second, that the ends of all rational beings must of necessity fit into a single universal, harmonious pattern, which some men are able to discern more clearly than others; third, that all conflict ... is due solely to the clash of reason with the irrational.
>
> *(154)*

He explains that the "rule of experts" comes from the argument (prominent in Plato) that my "real" self must be rational and "would" want me to obey the guardians or confess in a show trial or vote Republican—the general will and the social contract yet again. The expert, therefore, in my own real interest, issues the order for my death by firing squad. One is reminded of the procedures of the Spanish Inquisition, the very model of paternal expertise. When a Jew under torture had renounced his religion, he was baptized and immediately executed, as ready now to enter Paradise.

The best defense we have against bad arguments is the ability to see through the staging of the Nuremberg Rally or the doctoring of spin. Rhetorical self-consciousness—the ability to "toggle" between looking at and looking through a text, as the literary critic Richard Lanham puts it—is the best defense we have yet devised for what we value. It's a shabby thing by the standard of the Platonic forms or natural right, I admit, with their lovely if blinding uniformity of light. But it's all we've got.

Like democracy, which it defends, and the market, to which it runs parallel, rhetoric is the worst form of wisdom, except for those others that have been tried from time to time. In other words, if we break an argument into rhetoric and dialectic (here even Aristotle erred), the dialectic takes immediately a falsely superior position. Lanham's toggle is always off.

The move is assured by the long and lunatic fascination with certitude since the Pythagoreans showed by force of reason that not all numbers between 0 and 1 can be expressed as the ratio of two whole numbers. The actual human argument of law courts is downgraded to mere persuasion or politics or advertising or teaching or something else without the dignity of the Attic Greek construction for verbs of actual seeing. The actual human argument of scientific laboratories and blackboards is elevated to scientific method, beyond rhetorical scrutiny. (It is one reason for the Law of Academic Status: the most useful teaching, such as freshman English or education, has the lowest status, with offices down in the basement.) Philosophers and scientists, believing themselves in possession of certitude, never requiring a toggle, are encouraged to sneer. Planners and politicians, believing themselves in sight of utopia, are encouraged to ordain. It is not an encouragement either of them needs.

The missing ingredient in humane liberal thought, I am arguing, is rhetoric. As John of Salisbury wrote eight centuries ago in his defense: "Rhetoric is the beautiful and the fruitful union between reason and expression. Through harmony, it holds human communities together" (quoted in Vickers 1989, 30). The noncoercive act is persuasion, from Latin *suadeo*, having the same Indo-European root as English "sweet." The audience rule and are democratic. It is a matter of who's in charge. "Convince," on the other hand, means in Latin "defeat utterly."

The war-embittered men of the seventeenth century revived Plato's search for certitude. Putting Nature to the rack and proving theorems beyond excoriating doubt are the ambitions of men who would abandon harmonious persuasion in favor of a lonely and for the most part pointless certitude. In Hobbes's view, geometry was "the only Science that it hath pleased God hitherto to bestow on mankind" (Hobbes 1909–1914 [1651/1668], Chap. 4: Of Speech, 12). Free persuasion, by contrast, I have noted, following Adam Smith, shares numerous qualities with free exchange. Speech is a deal between the speaker and the audience. The authoritarians scorn it. Eric Hoffer, a San Francisco dockworker and sage, was walking back to the city after being paid off for some fruit-picking. As he tramped along the highway, wishing he was on a bus, he saw one coming a way off. No bus stop was in sight and his tattered clothing was not going to persuade the driver to stop. Inspired, he pulled out his fresh wad of dollar bills and waved them at the approaching bus. In good market-directed fashion, the driver stopped and took him to San Francisco. The money talked. He was persuasive. Not coercive.

Exchange is symbolic speech, protected in the ideal speech community. Persuasion and exchange share a unique feature as devices of altering other people's behavior, in that the people thus altered are *glad* the offer was made. Not so of coercion. It is not surprising to find aristocratic Plato equally outraged at the "flattery" of *hoi polloi* by democratic orators and at the taking of fees by the professors of oratory. In the *Republic*, he showed, consistent with his sneers at persuasion, that he was opposed to free exchange as well.

Liberty depends on—indeed is the same as—Habermas' ideal speech situation. Liberty has a rhetorical definition. It is why liberty of speech and liberty of expressions analogous to speech, such as offers of money or burnings of flags, are foundational. Academic life itself, which should approximate the ideal speech situation, commonly falls short of ideal liberty of speech. Bad rhetoric, such as those of mindless positivism, mindless Marxism, or mindless conservatism, block free inquiry (though by no physical coercion, usually). A good rhetoric conforms better than does modernist science or the other certitude-faiths to our shared vision of the good society, conforming better to pluralism and the negative liberty that defends it. Machinery for the making of constitutions and the revealing of preferences lack point if the society in which they are installed is one in which honest rhetoric is made impossible. If no one can be persuaded, we are alone.

What is most wrong with Charles Taylor's argument against negative liberty and with similar arguments by people after Mill appropriating the title of liberal but adopting illiberal rhetoric is that it is an end-state theory of liberty rather than a procedural theory. It focuses on what people come to be at the end of the game rather than on the ethics by which they can change themselves along the way. One might reply, so much the better for modem left progressivism: it gets right to the point, achieving at a stroke the desirable end state, positive liberty, launching direct wars on poverty. But it gets to the point in the same sense that state-provided education gets to the point. Is there an argument that education makes better humans? Well, then, let the government provide it. Such a statistical conclusion does not of course follow (as Milton Friedman so long argued, and since the 1990s the Swedes have agreed).

Taylor laments that we lose in the liberal, negative, physical-coercion definition of liberty "some of the most inspiring terrain of liberalism, which is concerned with individual self-realization" (Taylor 1979, 193). I wish left progressives would rethink their affection for such terrain, in view of its consequences in demoralizing the poor and enriching the rich. Hardnosed political economists want to get beyond reason and speech, which they view as mere verbiage, to something more real underneath. The real, they think, will be manipulable, the levers of history. The point, they say, is not to say, but to change it. The words of politics are just talk. We Marxians or anti-Marxians know that talk means nothing. When I hear the word "talk" I reach for my wallet.

On the contrary, though, talk is the main asset of a political culture, as durable as any of its bronze and pyramids. When "words lost their meaning," the Athenians were doomed (White 1984). Indeed, institutions consist largely of ethical agreements good or bad about how to talk—addressing all remarks to the Speaker of the House or sticking with the corporate team or professors scorning, or students shouting, who will not articulate their reasons. Markets, in particular, live on people's tongues, which, therefore, must be free to wag. A calculation of the amount of time business people spend talking to suppliers, employees, bankers, customers, and each other has shown that the economy is largely a rhetorical affair, a matter of establishing ethos and in other ways persuading each other to cooperate (Klamer and McCloskey 1995). "Changing minds," we say, but by no violence.

Smith, the professor of rhetoric in the defense of liberty, opined that the propensity to truck and barter is "as seems more probable, ... the necessary consequence of the faculties of reason and speech" (Smith [1776] 1976, 14; Chap. 2, Glasgow edition, 25). The line was no throw-away. In *The Theory of Moral Sentiments*, he carries on the analysis which in *The Wealth of Nations* belonged not to his subject to inquire:

> The desire of being believed, the desire of persuading, of leading and directing other people, seems to be one of the strongest of all our natural desires. It is, perhaps, the instinct upon which is founded the faculty of speech, the characteristic faculty of human nature.
>
> *(Smith 1982 [1759/1790], 336)*

Frank Knight wrote in 1944 that

> If men are to think critically and yet escape moral skepticism and a destructive relativism, they must have faith, on some ground, in the validity of thought and discussion. ... Nothing properly called absolute truth is possible. ... The highest certainty, beyond the direct awareness that thinking is a free activity, is that it takes place in social beings living in a social milieu, i.e., in connection with discussion.
>
> *("The Rights of Man and Natural Law," 295–296)*

Such an emphasis on discussion and rhetoric is not, I repeat, anti-realist, or against smaller reality. The earth is still an oblate spheroid and the table still stands against the wall. But realism does not entail attributing nothing to the way we talk about politics or the economy. *Realpolitik* is not entailed by realism. It is a naive realist who thinks that being one requires him to scorn ideas. At the end of his *Dialogus*, written a century and a half or so after the death of the Roman Republic, Tacitus has the anti-democrat Maternus assert that

> great and notable oratory is the foster-child of license (which fools call liberty), the companion of sedition, a goad to the unbridled masses. ... It does not arise in well constituted states. What Spartan orator have we heard of? ... Among the Macedonians or the Persians, or any race who have been content under settled rule, eloquence has been unknown. ... The Athenians had a great many orators ... and among them the people ruled. ... Why bother with tedious orations to the mob when on matters of public policy it is not the ignorant many who deliberate but that One, the emperor, who is most wise?
>
> *(38: 2–4)*

True enough. Three cheers then for license, sedition, and the unbridled masses, if the alternative is Sparta, Imperial Rome, or the People's Republic of China. A healthy tyranny, with nothing to be argued about, and no ideas to be concluded in the forum by mutual agreement, could dispense with the services of a Demosthenes, a Cicero, a Daniel Webster, or a Vaclav Havel, or for that matter Steve Jobs. When the government is well constituted and its subjects are obedient, rhetoric and a free economy can die.

That puts the point of humane liberalism well.

Digging Deeper

Discussion Questions

1. Do you agree that markets are communicative at heart?
2. Given the importance of communication in democracy, how do markets play into democratic ideals?

Suggested Further Reading

Duerringer, C. M. (2018). Research in the rhetoric of economics: a critical review. *Review of Communication*, 18(4), 284–300.

Note

1 A longer version of the essay was "The Rhetoric of Liberty." *Rhetoric Society Quarterly* 26 (1, 1996): pp. 9–27. A revised version, longer than the version presented here, was published in Roger E. Bissell, Chris Matthew Sciabarra, & Edward W. Younkins, eds. *The Dialectics of Liberty: Exploring the Context of Human Freedom* (Lexington Books 2019).

References

Berlin, I. (1969 [1958]). Two concepts of liberty. In I. Berlin (Ed.), *Four Essays on Liberty* (pp. 118–172). New York: Oxford University Press 1969.

Hobbes, T. (1909–1914 [1651/1668]). Of man, being the first part of *Leviathan*. In *The Harvard Classics*. Selected by Charles W. Eliot. New York: P. F. Collier & Sons. Online at: http://www.bartleby.com/34/5/4.html.

Klamer, A., and McCloskey, D. N. (1995). One quarter of GDP is persuasion. *American Economic Review*, 85(May), 191–195.

Knight, F. (1936 [1947]). Pragmatism and social action. In *Freedom and Reform* (pp. 35–44).

———. (1944 [1947]). The rights of man and natural law. In *Freedom and Reform* (pp. 262–300).

Lincoln, A. (1864). Address at a sanitary fair. Baltimore. April 18. At http://teachingamericanhistory.org/library/document/address-at-a-sanitary-fair/.

Macaulay, T. B. (1830 [1881]). Southey's colloquies. *Edinburgh Review*, reprinted 1860 in *Macaulay's Essays* (pp. 132–187). Boston, MA: Riverside Edition, 1881, vol. I, Chap. ii.

McCloskey, D. N. (2016). *Bourgeois equality: How ideas, not capital or institutions, enriched the world*. Chicago: University of Chicago Press.

Partridge, P. H. (1967). Freedom. In P. Edwards (Ed.), *The Encyclopedia of Philosophy* (pp. 3222–3223). London and New York: Macmillan.

Plato. (1997). *Plato: Complete Works*. Edited with Introduction and Notes by J. M. Cooper. Indianapolis, IN: Hackett Publishing. Of which *Sophist* (pp. 235–293), translated by N. P. White; *Phaedru* (pp. 506–556), translated by A. Neymanas, and P. Woodruff; *Gorgias* (pp. 791–869), translated by D. J. Zeyl.

Smith, A. (1982 [1759/1790]). *The Theory of Moral Sentiments*. Glasgow edition. Edited by D. D. Raphael, and A. L. Macfie. Oxford: Oxford University Press.

———. (1978, 1982 [1762–1763, 1766]). *Lectures on Jurisprudence*. Glasgow edition. Edited by R. L. Meek, D. D. Raphael, and P. G. Stein. Oxford: Oxford University Press.

———. (1976 [1776]). *An Inquiry into the Nature and Causes of the Wealth of Nations* (Vol. 1). Glasgow edition. Edited by R. H. Campbell, A. S. Skinner, and W. B. Todd. Oxford: Oxford University Press.

Taylor, C. (1979). What's wrong with negative liberty. In A. Ryan (Ed.), *The Idea of Freedom: Essays in Honor of Isaiah Berlin* (pp. 175–193). Oxford: Oxford University Press.

Taylor, M. (1982). *Community, Anarchy, and Liberty*. New York: Cambridge University Press.

Vickers, B. (1989). *In Defense of Rhetoric*. Oxford: Clarendon Press.

White, J. B. (1984). *When Words Lose Their Meaning: Constitutions and Reconstitutions of Language, Character, and Community*. Chicago, IL: University of Chicago Press.

INDEX

Printed in the United States
by Baker & Taylor Publisher Services